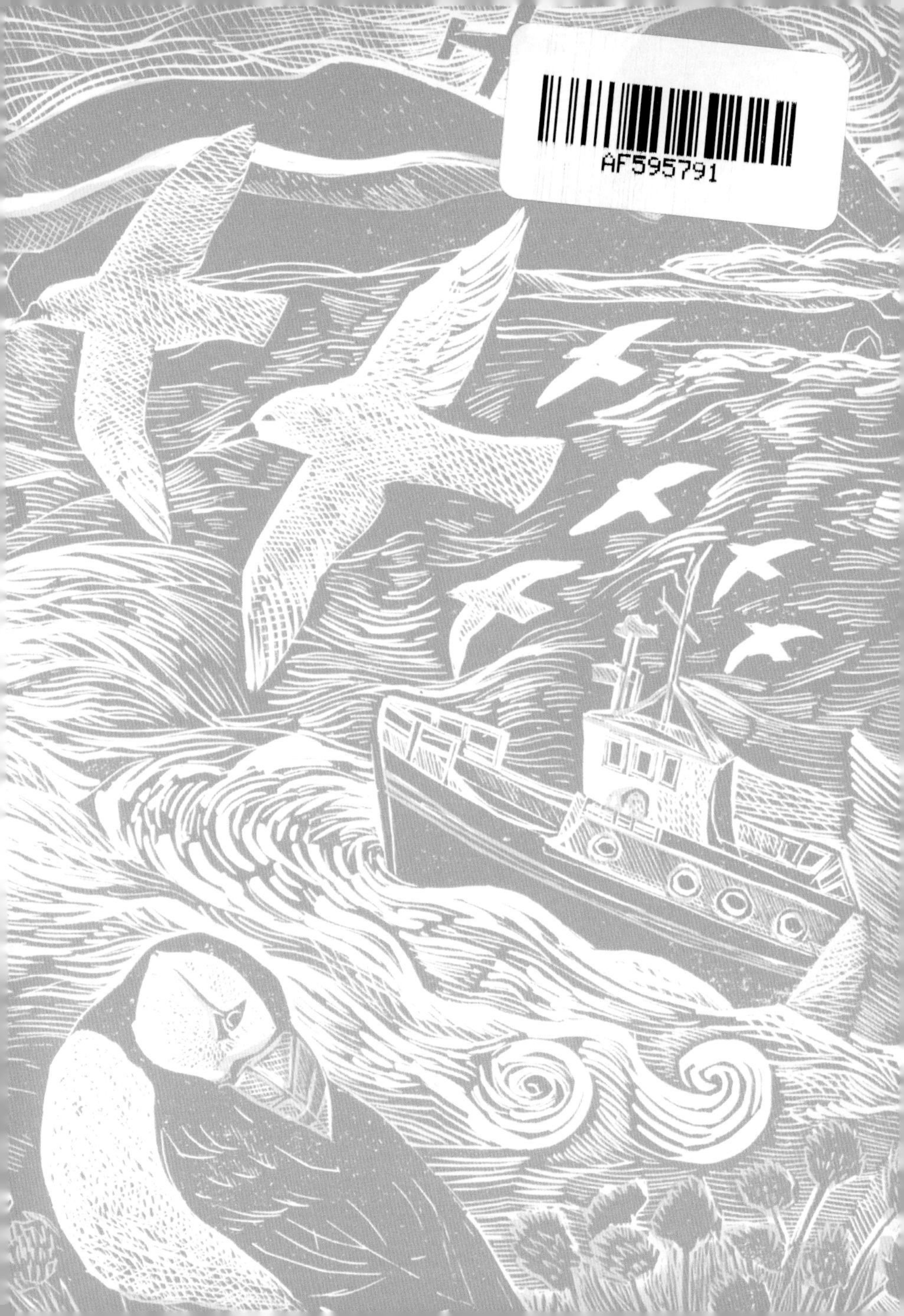

SUMMER'S HUM

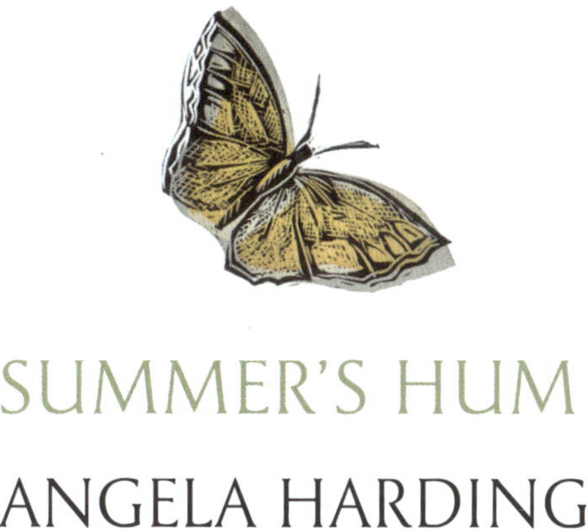

SUMMER'S HUM

ANGELA HARDING

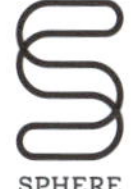

SPHERE

SPHERE

First published in Great Britain in 2025 by Sphere
1 3 5 7 9 10 8 6 4 2

A CIP catalogue for this book is available from the British Library.

ISBN 9781408721933

Project Editor: Helen Brocklehurst
Production Manager: Abby Marshall
Cover and interior design: Ben Prior
Typeset in Spectral Light
Printed in Italy by Printer Trento Srl
Papers used by Sphere are from well-managed forests and other responsible sources.

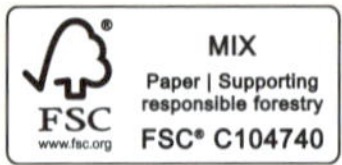

Sphere
An imprint of
Little, Brown Book Group
Carmelite House
50 Victoria Embankment
London EC4Y 0DZ

The authorised representative
in the EEA is
Hachette Ireland
8 Castlecourt Centre
Dublin 15, D15 XTP3, Ireland
(email: info@hbgi.ie)

An Hachette UK Company
www.hachette.co.uk
www.littlebrown.co.uk

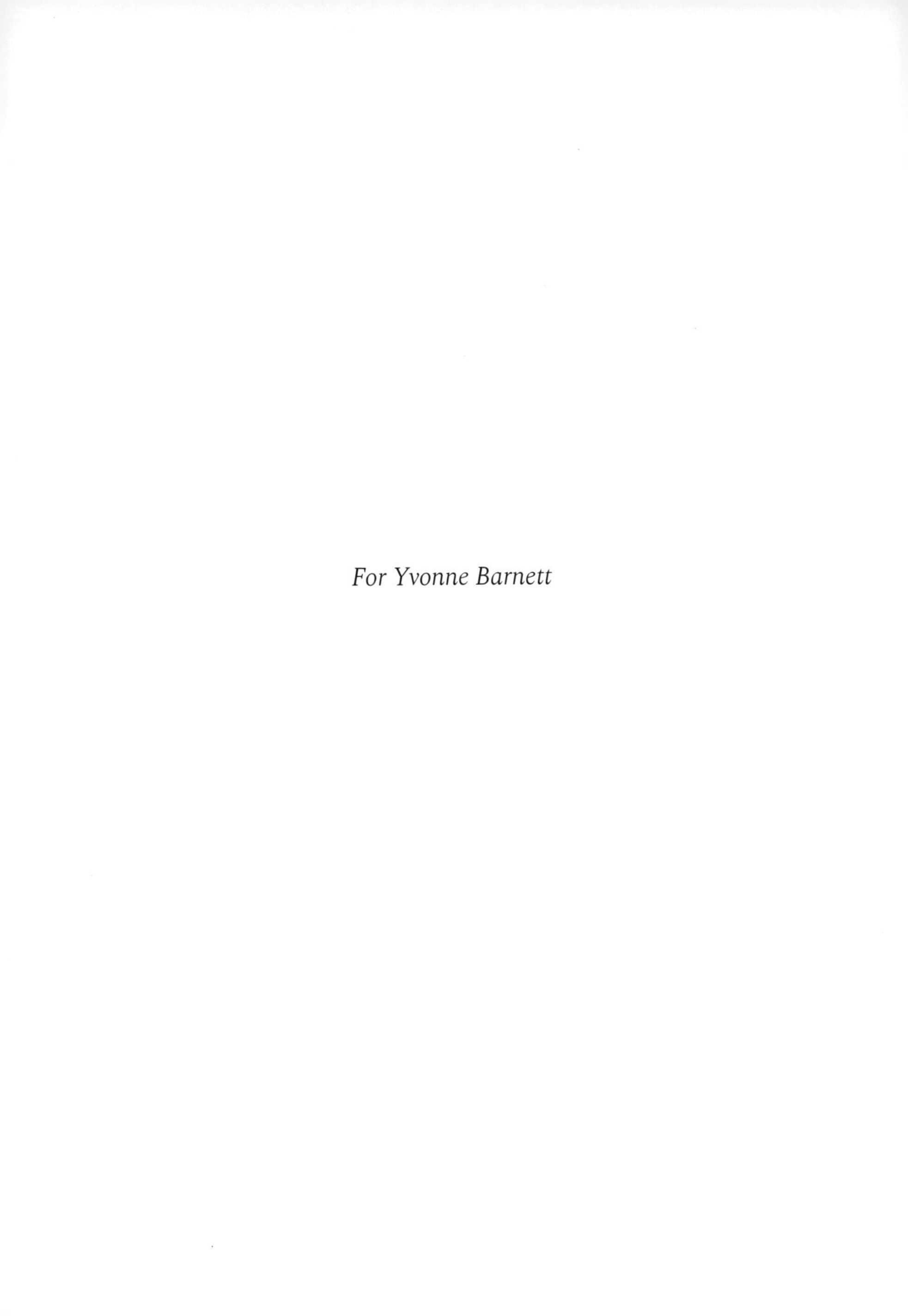

For Yvonne Barnett

Introduction

Summer is a time of changing colours and changing light. It is when the sharp acid green of spring growth deepens and darkens. Lengthening days and stronger light bring change to our garden; it is transformed into a tapestry of colour. The wildflower bank outside my window hums and buzzes. These insects feed on pink and white campion, cornflowers, speedwell, scarlet pimpernel and poppies. At midday the summer sun spreads the perfume of rose and honeysuckle to every corner, bees become drowsy and drunk on these scents. It is then, when the days are long, the garden becomes a place of drama and summer hums.

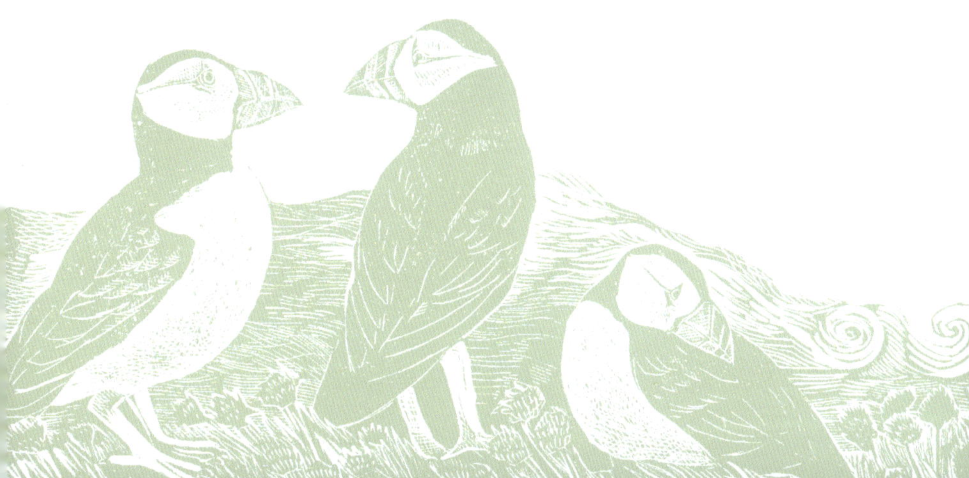

In fine weather, the evening garden glows; it is bathed in a soft, orange light and made more beautiful still by blackbird song. A male blackbird tops the walnut tree; he sings to announce his presence. It is a beautiful melody that spills out from him – rolling, burbling notes that mark his territory. This walnut tree was planted by my husband, Mark, many years ago. It is a favourite singing post for lots of birds but it's the blackbird that seems to own it. In summer he sings from its branches at first light, and then again at the end of the day. The bird becomes a silhouette against the dusky sky, signalling that the day is done.

Outside the garden, the colour of the surrounding countryside also changes. The leaves of the oak trees turn to a soft olive, veined with darker green and edged in mustard. These leaves already carry the marks of a spring gone and of summer's heat. The oak trees edge the sheep fields that I look out on from my studio, forming canopies of shade for the sheep. On hot days, the flock shelters under the welcome, leafy shadows and looks like a Samuel Palmer painting. On rainy days, they sit closely together in one sheep-shaped huddle, protected from the rain and wind.

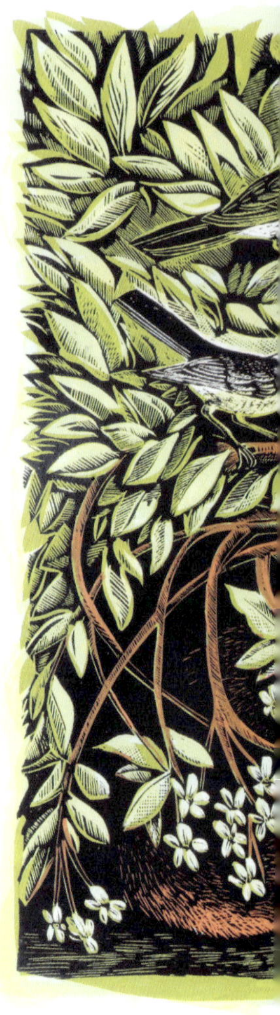

Above:
Summer Foxes at Marske Hall
(Linocut and silkscreen)

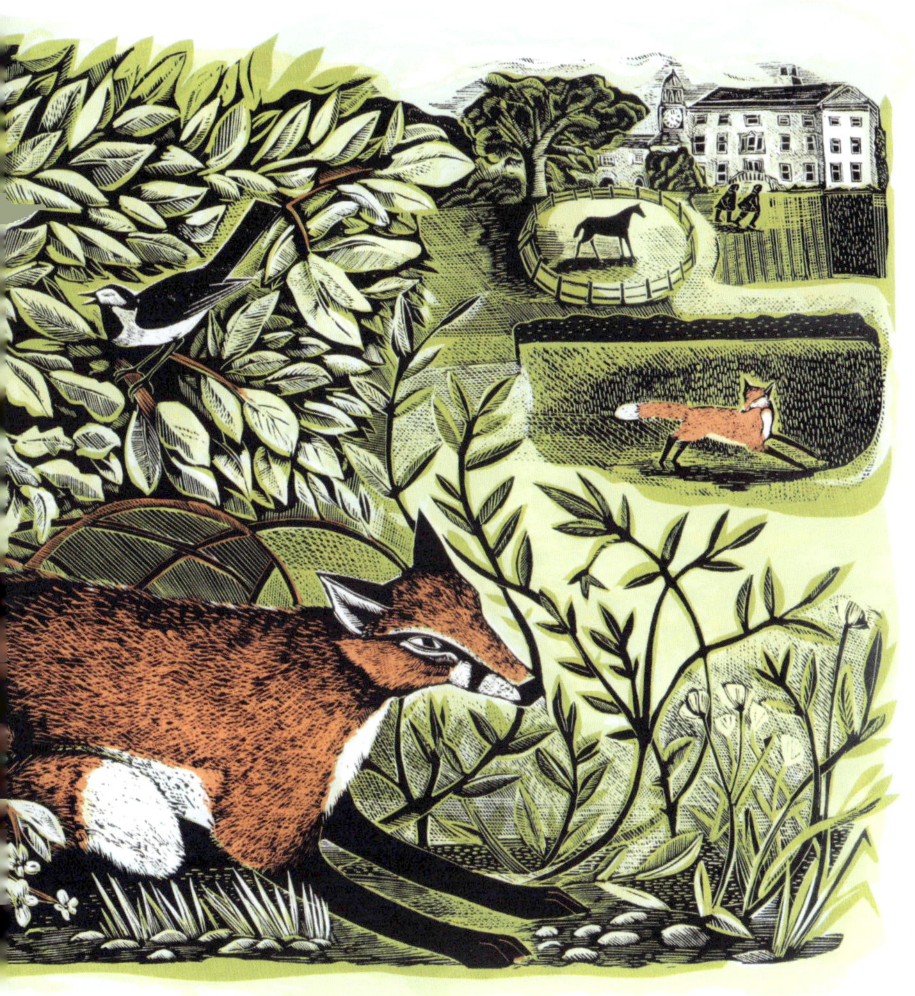

Early summer is the start of our slightly nomadic lifestyle. During the summer months Mark and I take full advantage of owning a small, wooden sailing boat. *Windsong* was built in the 1970s for the Essex rivers and has a lifting keel. Her low draft in the water allows us to visit both rivers and coast. We often go north, sailing up the east coast of the UK from Suffolk to Shetland. If the weather allows, Mark stops en route at Fair Isle. Fair Isle is the halfway point between Orkney and Shetland, a small island three miles by one and a half miles. It is a place both Mark and I love to visit. The wildlife is astounding: puffins, gannets, seals and wading birds of all types. Many of the watery images in this book are a direct response to visiting these islands and travelling this coastline.

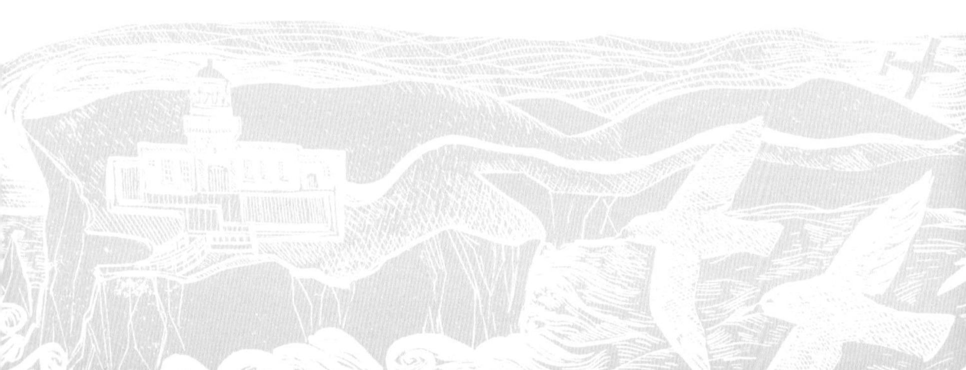

Summer's Hum is the second in a series of four books that reflect on the seasons. This quartet has its origins in my first book, *A Year Unfolding*, which is a printmaker's view of the changing seasons. In *Summer's Hum* I have added new images and text to my original thoughts about summer. This book is a new format; a small book that you can put in your pocket to muse on travels and in quiet moments, or a gift book to cherish with others who share my love of nature. The other books in this series are *Spring Unfurled*, *Falling into Autumn* and *Winter's Song*.

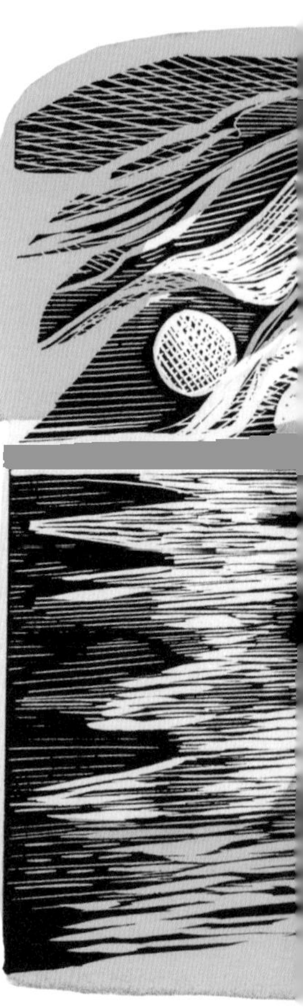

When on the Butley river, our boat *Windsong* is held in place by a buoy, not moored to a pontoon. So to get to shore and back, we use the tender. Leaving the boat in early evening, it is a short row ashore and then a three-mile walk to Orford. We do this on the evenings we eat out, which is a real treat. The treat is not only a lovely meal, but watching the wildlife as we walk to Orford and come back through the dark. The sandy path is lit by moonlight, creating strange, silver shadows that make you feel unnerved. As you walk past the farms, old cars and tractors – that nature has reclaimed as places to nest in and hide within – loom out from the dark.

Above:
A Suffolk Night Walk
(Linocut and silkscreen)

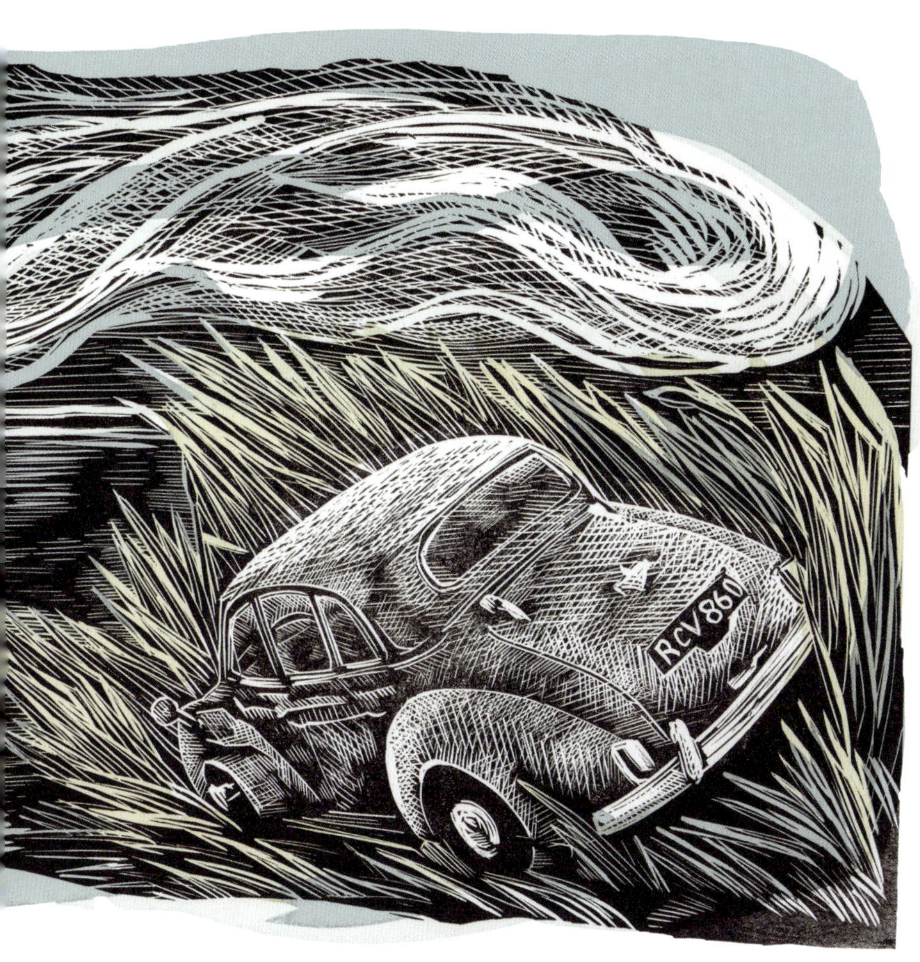
RCV 860

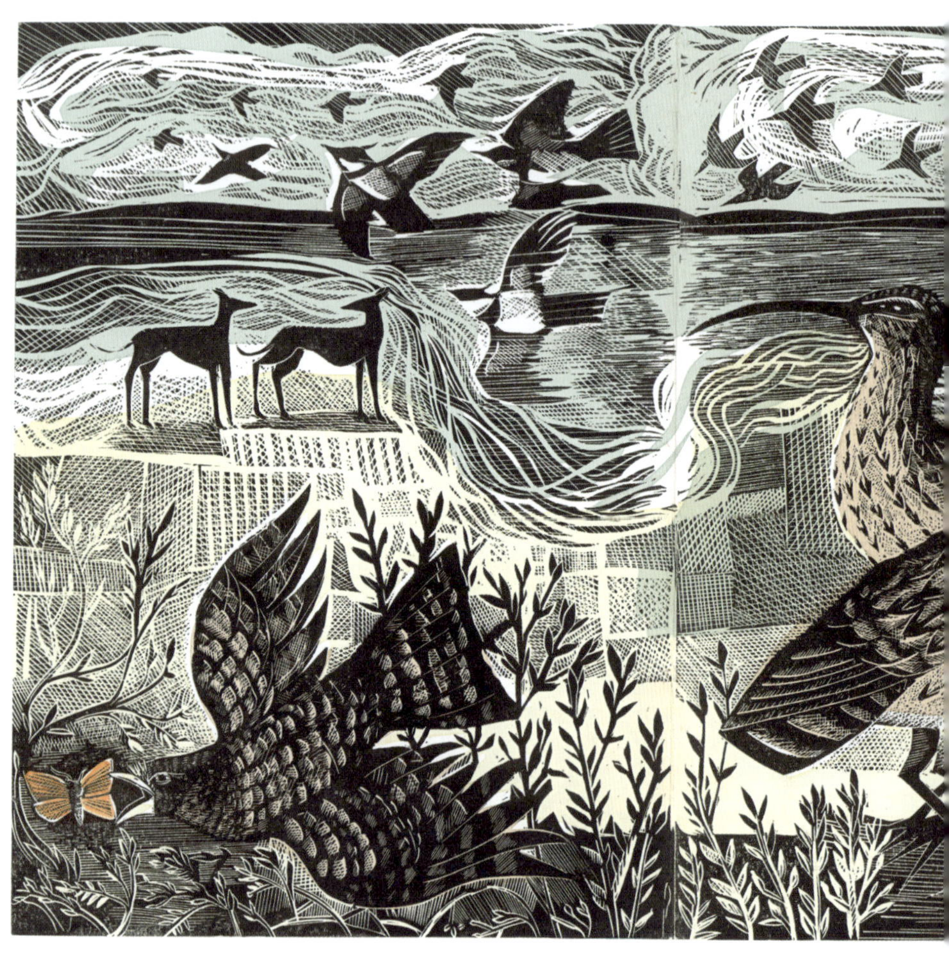

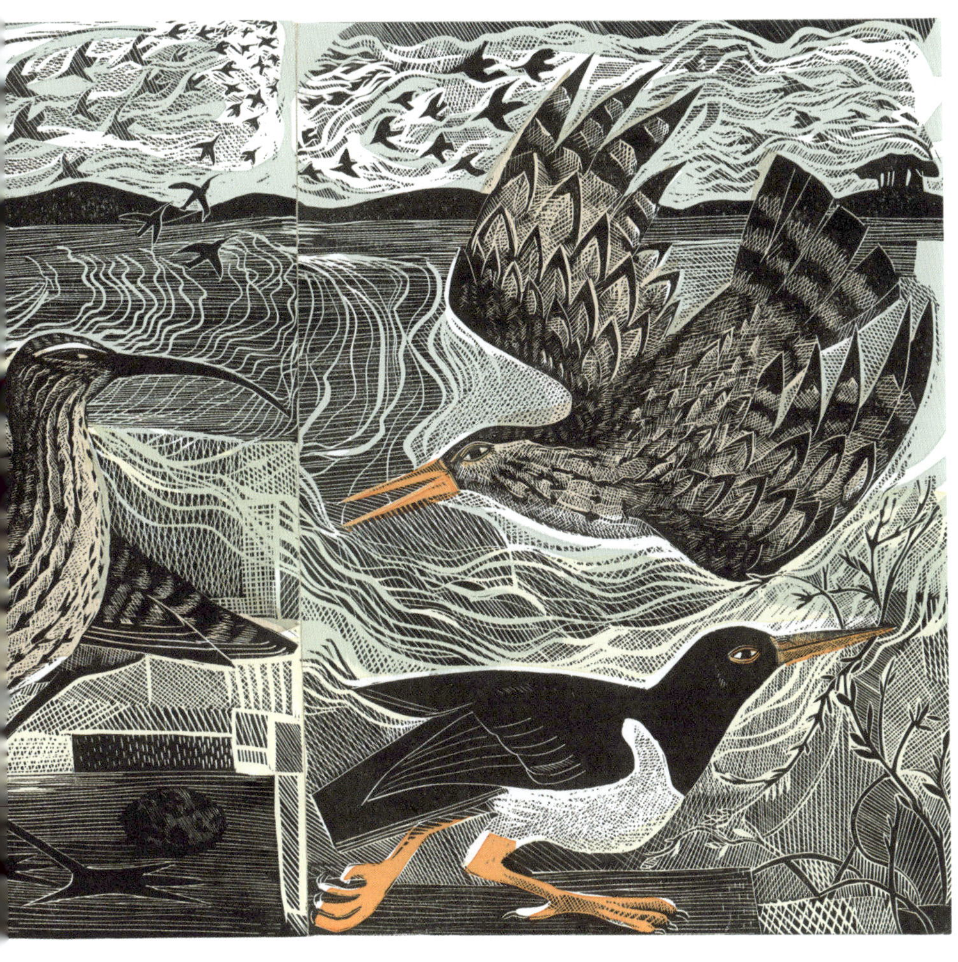

Above:
Suffolk Coastline
(Linocut and
silkscreen)

The garden is always in need of some attention in the summer. As we are away for so much of the season, I do not grow many edibles, but a section of the garden is laid down to raised beds that have always been intended to be used as a kitchen garden. There are strawberries, artichokes, bronze fennel, red and blackcurrants. Though these are intended for our table they are mainly eaten by the birds. I know you can net them, but I think the birds need them more than we do!

Opposite:
Butterflies and Flowers
(Linocut and silkscreen)

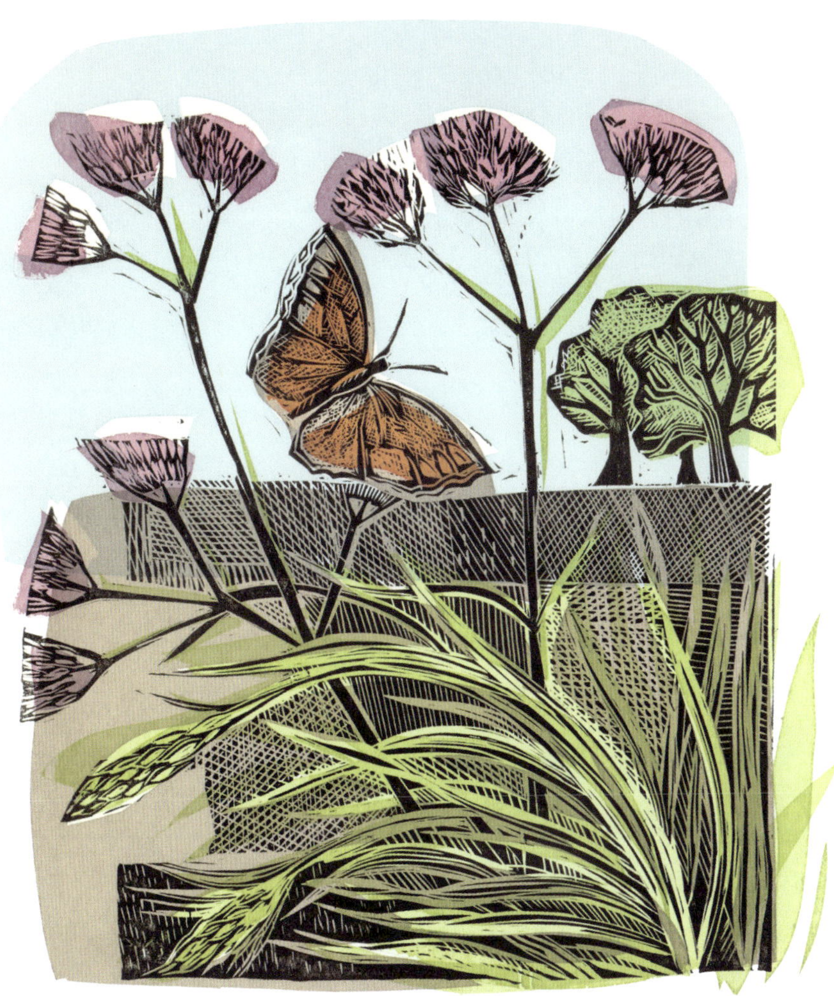

A regular summer stop on Windsong is visiting Snape Maltings in Suffolk.

Opposite:
Young Hare at Snape
(Linocut and silkscreen)

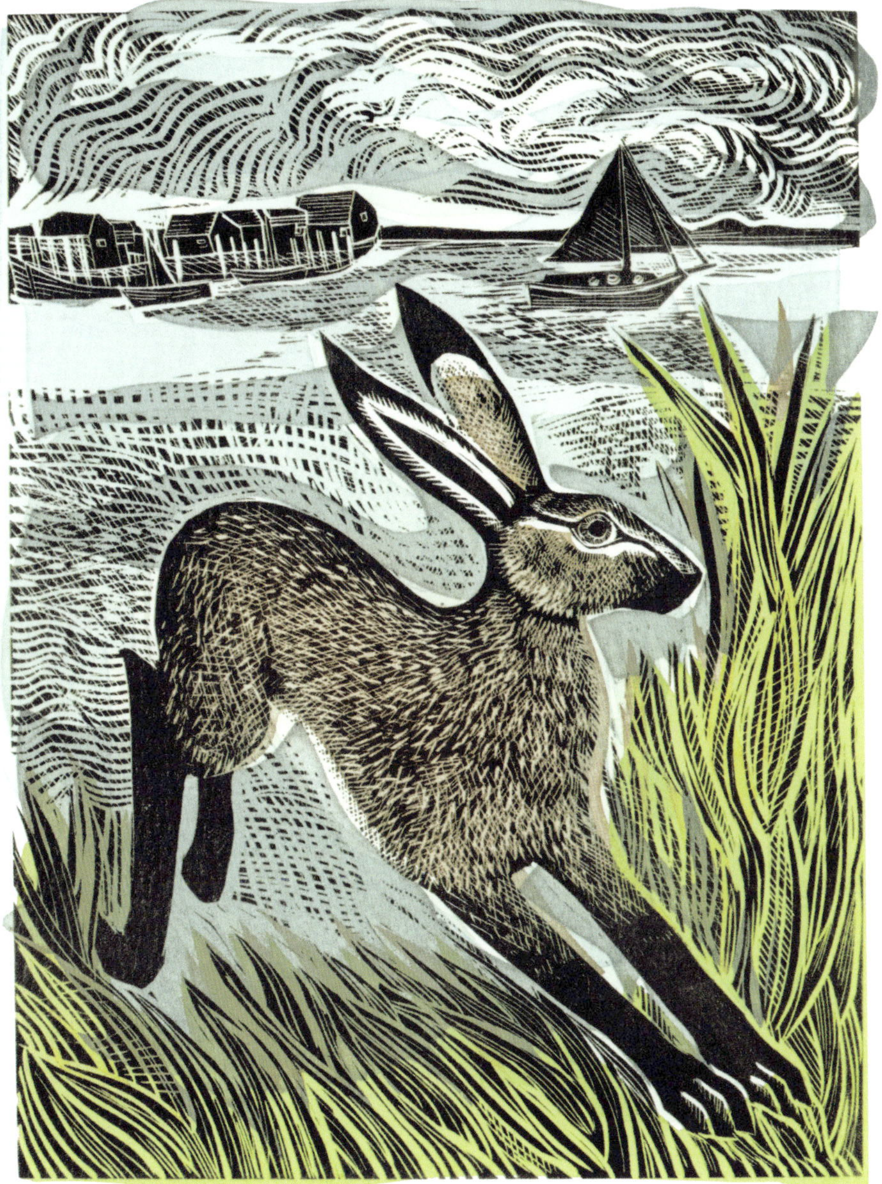

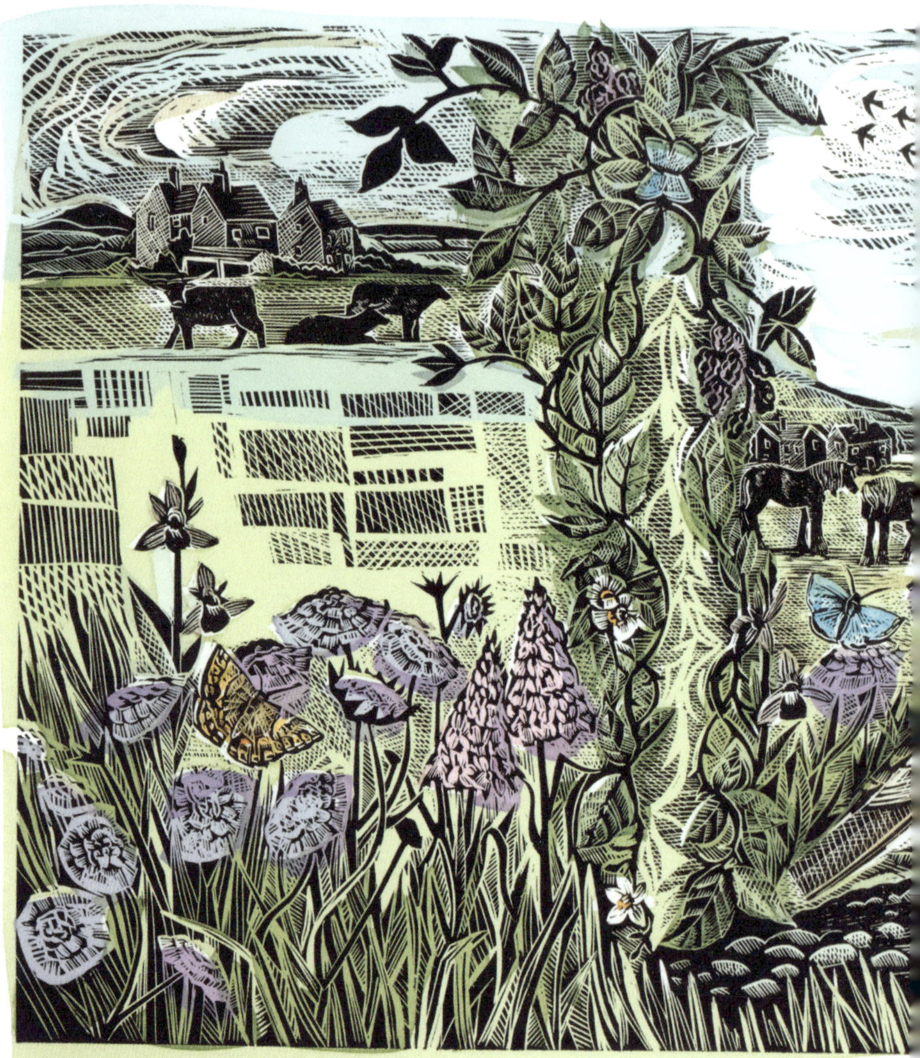

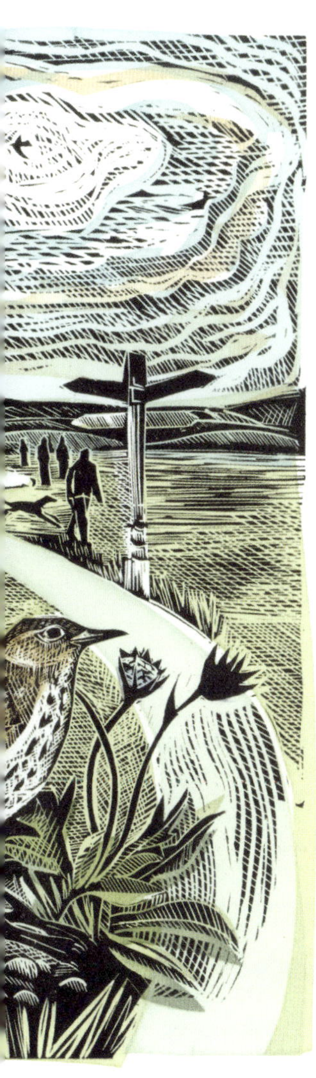

The Common, close to Minchinhampton in Gloucester, is a curious place as it seems to be both town and country at once. The road cuts across the chalk landscape which is home to orchids, rare blue butterflies, meadow pipits and cattle. All seem at home with the fact they live in a commuter belt.

Opposite:
The Common
(Linocut and silkscreen)

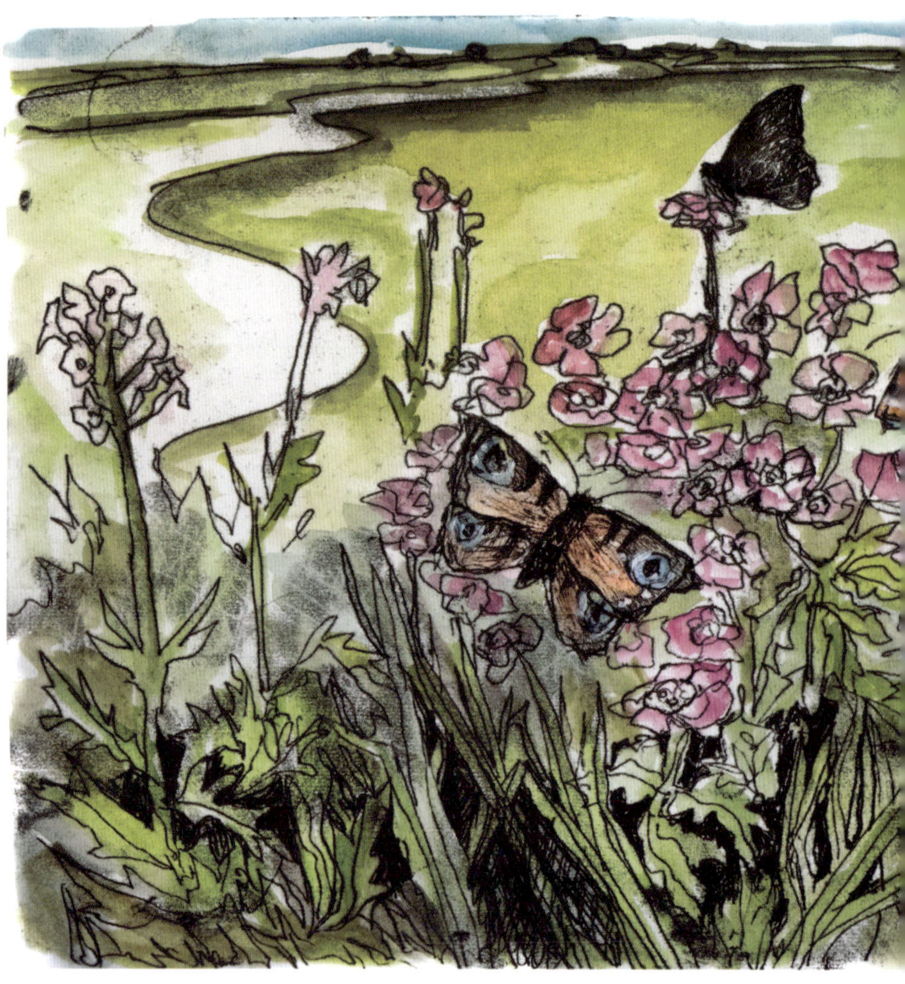

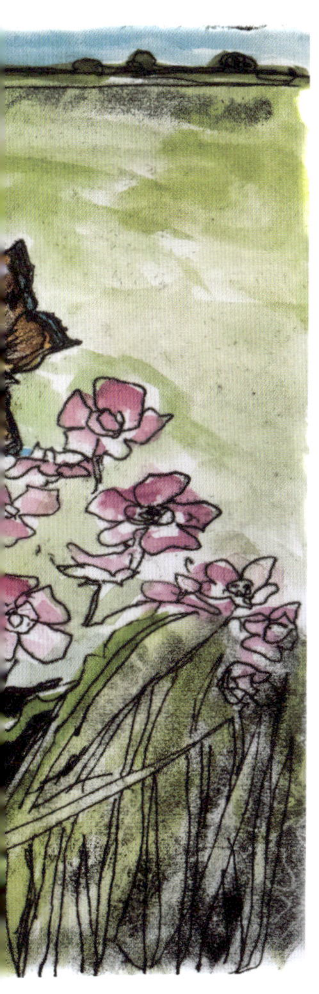

Midday sun sends much of nature searching for shade and many birds and animals take cover until later in the day. But other parts of nature seek out this time of day. Bees, butterflies and flowers soak up the heat to build up their energy supplies. The colours of high summer are sun-bleached: the greens of the garden and the hedgerows are faded sap green, the shadows cast are sharp-edged.

Opposite:
High Light
(Mono printing)

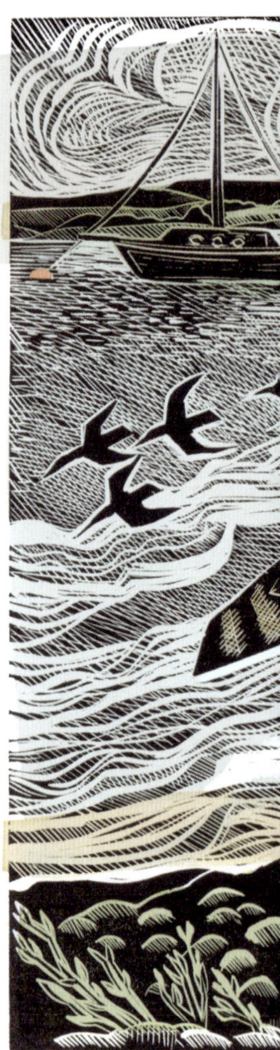

I have made many prints that feature curlews – their beautiful shape inspires me. Martlesham Creek is a small inlet of water on the river Deben; it is tree-lined, in a steep valley and is where we overwinter *Windsong*. The creek is a natural shelter, very different from being out in the open river. We do have a summer buoy in the middle of the Deben. It is rather underused as we move around the coast so much. But I love to spend time on the river. It is a much calmer experience than being out at sea. The Deben has great character, with its abandoned wooden fishing boats, now reclaimed by the river. They are creature-like, their exposed wooden ribs broken by the comings and goings of this wide, tidal river.

Opposite:
Two Curlews
(Linocut and silkscreen)

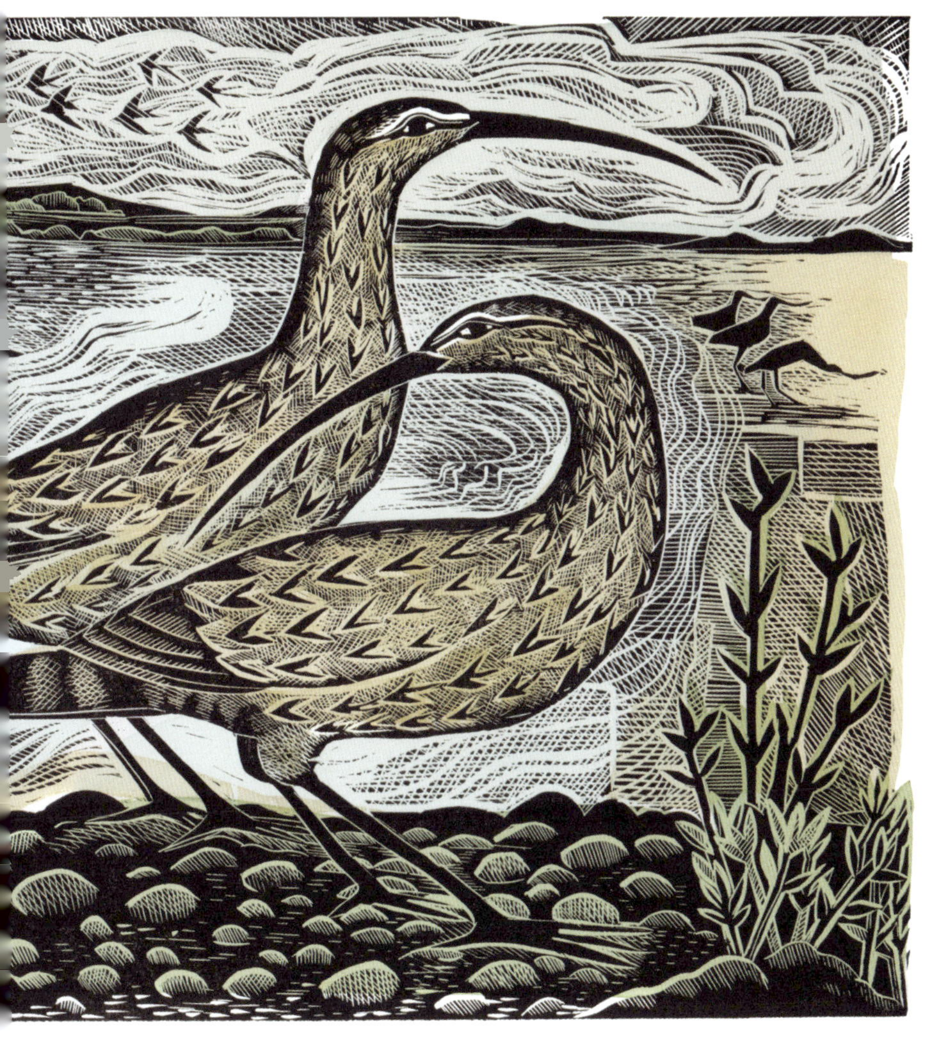

Orkney is a group of islands five miles off the north coast of Scotland. These islands are almost treeless and set in a windswept landscape edged with raging seas. Due to the constant strong winds, the plant life has adapted to growing low to the ground. One of these low-growing plants is the Orkney Pink. It forms small mounds of evergreen foliage; in springtime it is dotted with bright pink flowers. In this illustration I have combined the bright flowers with ringed plovers, a shoreline bird that darts in and out of breaking waves.

Opposite:
Plovers and Pinks
(Linocut and silkscreen)

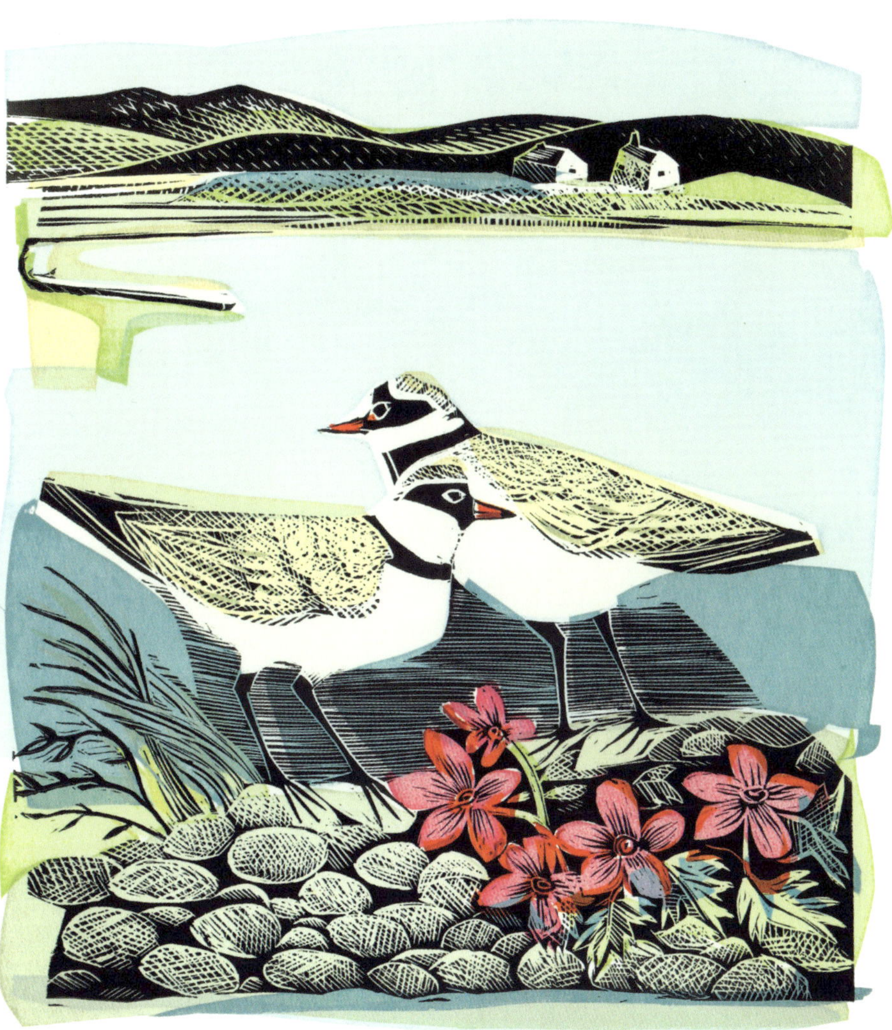

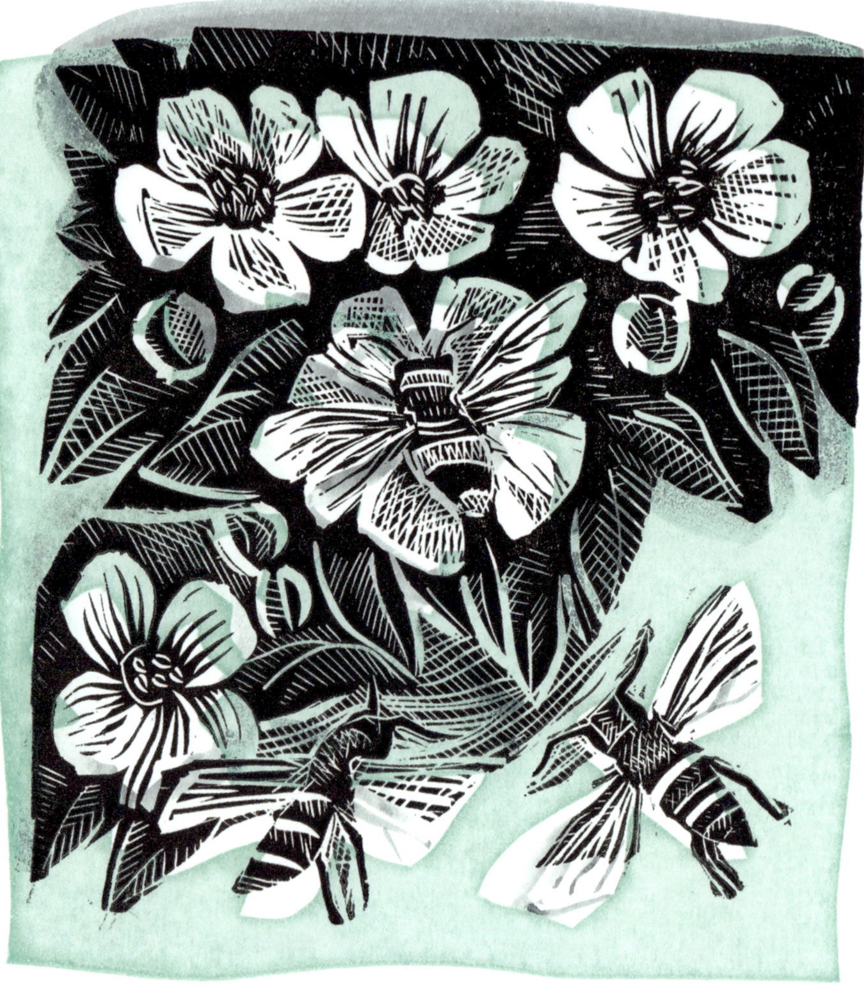

Bees, butterflies and flowers soak up the midday heat to build up their energy supplies.

Opposite:
Bees and Blossom
(Linocut and silkscreen)

There are some books that remain with us long after we have finished reading them. For me, J. A. Baker's *The Peregrine* is one of these books. Baker was a rare person; he was a true nature writer. In his writing he demonstrated both his formidable knowledge of the bird and a unique sense of place. Baker spent many winters tracking peregrines in the Essex countryside, noting their behaviour. He then distilled 10 years of notebooks in one book, *The Peregrine*. There is no question that the hours and hours of observation have been distilled into a unique piece of writing that is both poetic and scientific. I have not seen peregrines in Essex but mainly in Cornwall. I have watched them stoop, which is when they fold back their wings, falling at great speed to hit their prey. A breathtaking moment – then, the bird is gone, off to some other part of the cliffs to chase down rock pigeons and other small birds.

Opposite:
Two Falcons Watching
(Linocut)

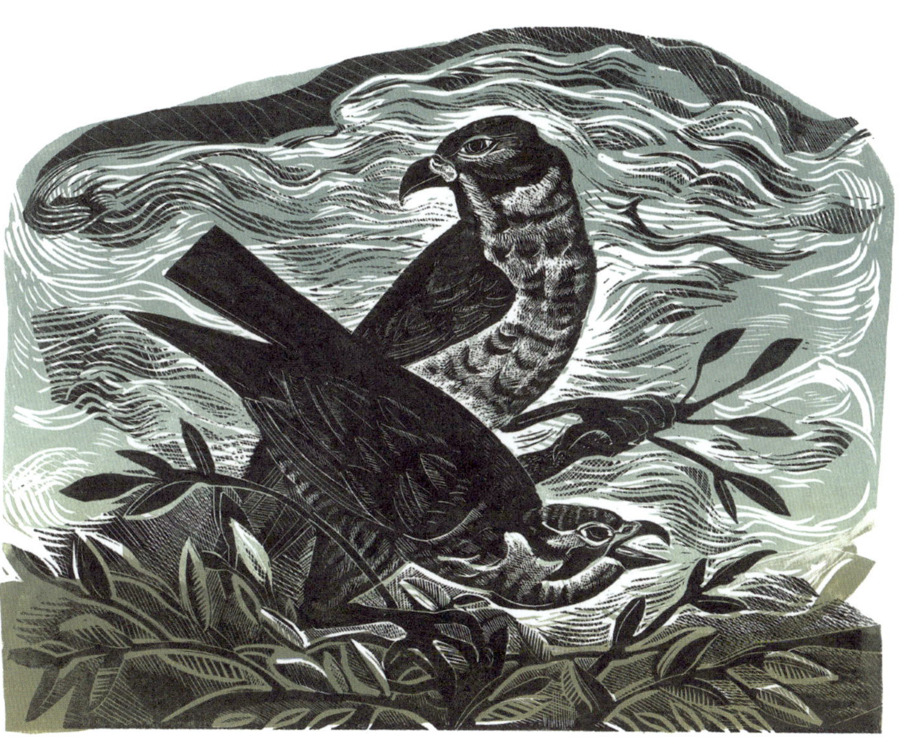

Poetry has always inspired my work. It was introduced to me, not by school, but by my father, Stephen Harding. He studied English literature at Cambridge under Professor Leavis in the late 1940s. I am very far from having great literary knowledge but the poems he read to me have always stayed close to my heart. In many of my prints you can see my father in the background – usually as a silhouette. He was a great walker, so he is often the small figure with his walking stick in hand. You can see him in *Visitors for Tea*; he too was a whipppet lover as well as a great tea drinker.

Opposite:
Vistors for Tea
(Linocut and silkscreen)

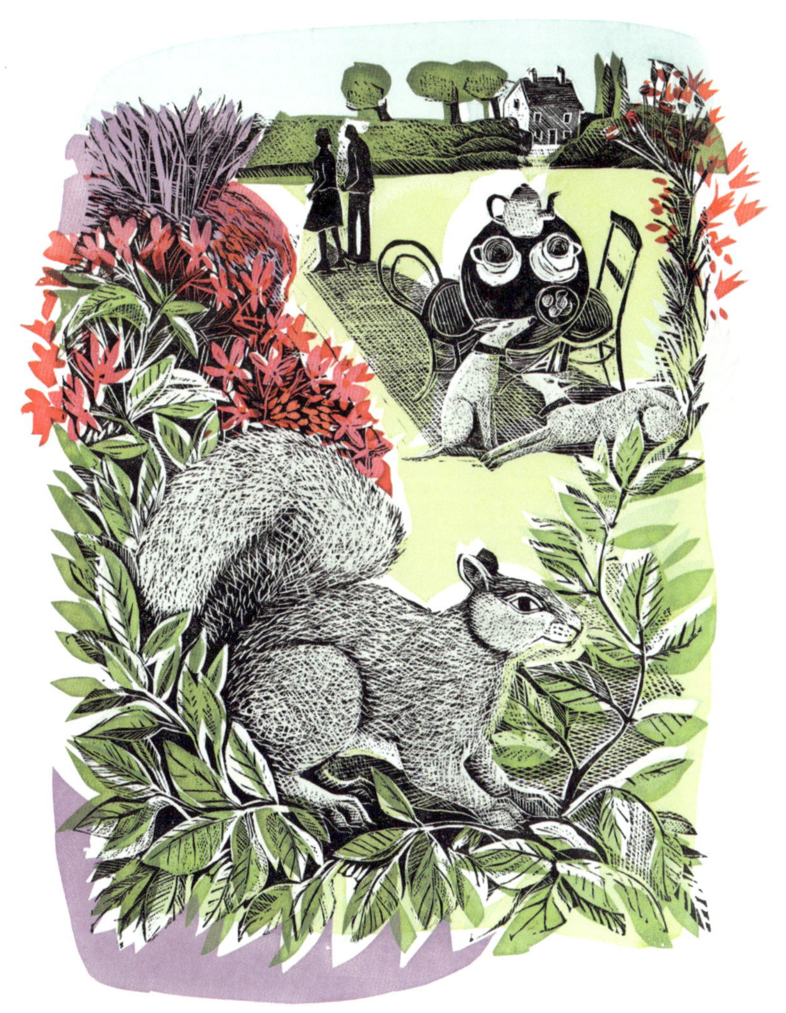

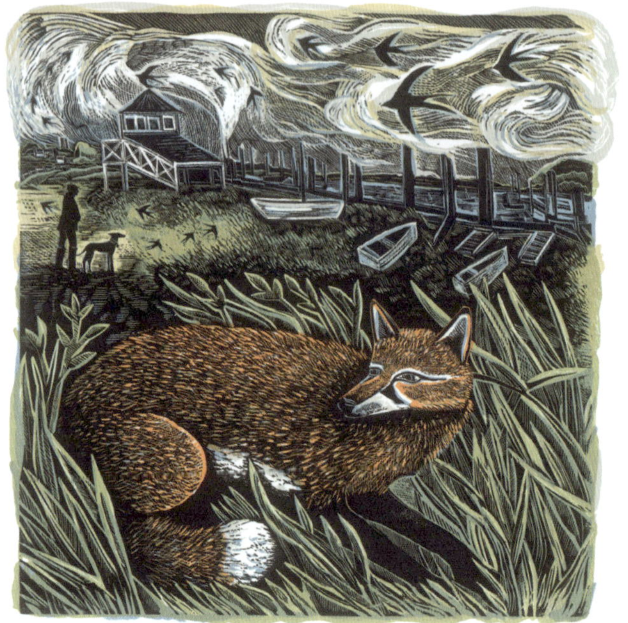

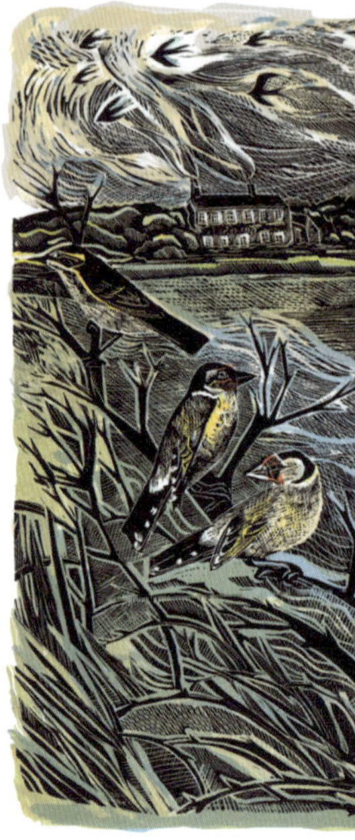

Together these pictures form my version of the path between Blakeney and Stiffkey, reflecting the parts of the coastal path I enjoy the most and find most memorable. The three prints can hang together or be seen as individual images. Each one reflects a different time of day from morning to dusk. *Morston Fox* is the first in this series.

Above:
North Norfolk Coastline Triptych
(Silkscreen print)

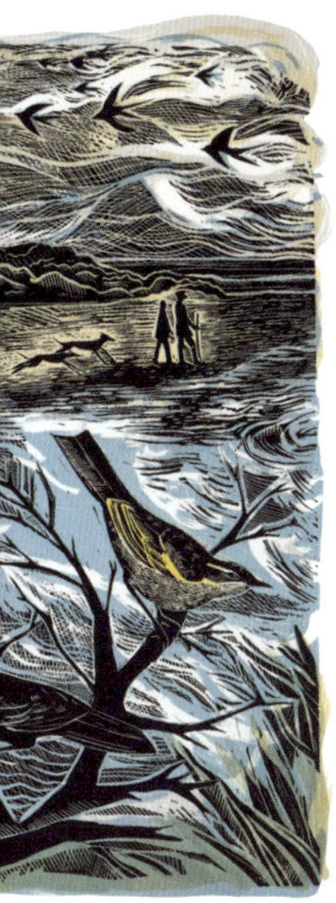

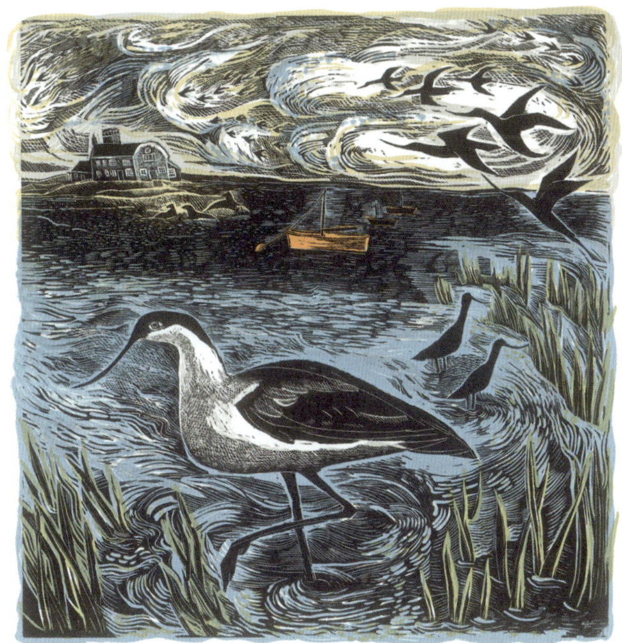

The early summer morning, when there can be a cloak of mist, is the perfect camouflage for an opportunistic fox. The second, *Church Cottage Morston* is about memories of setting out to walk in the high light of midday. Finally, *Avocets at Blakeney* is evening time when the low light sends long shadows across the marsh.

Living in Rutland, our nearest coast is north Norfolk. Before the days of working as a freelance professional artist, when I had to work for others, Mark and I would often drive to Norfolk for an evening walk. It was well worth the two-hour drive to smell the salty air and hear the curlews calling in a Norfolk sky.

Opposite:
Norfolk Still Life
(Linocut and silkscreen)

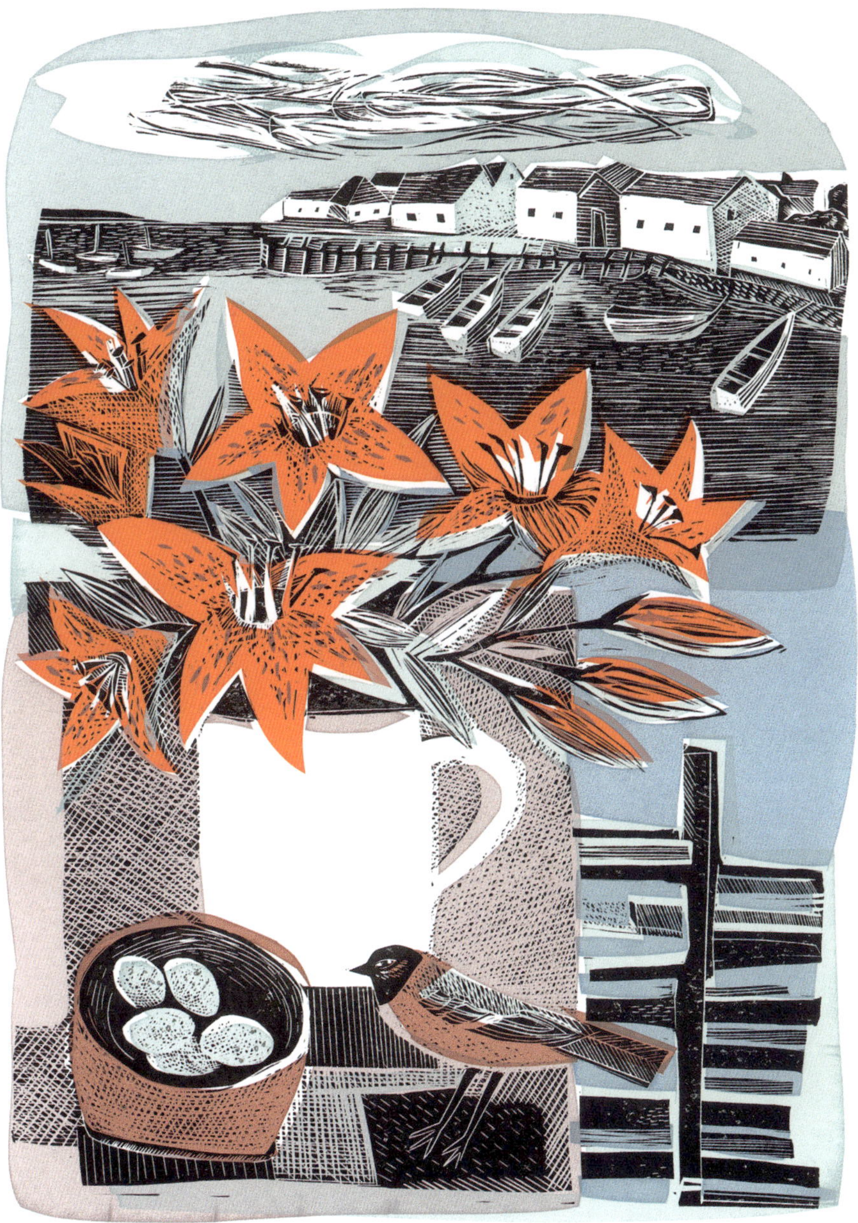

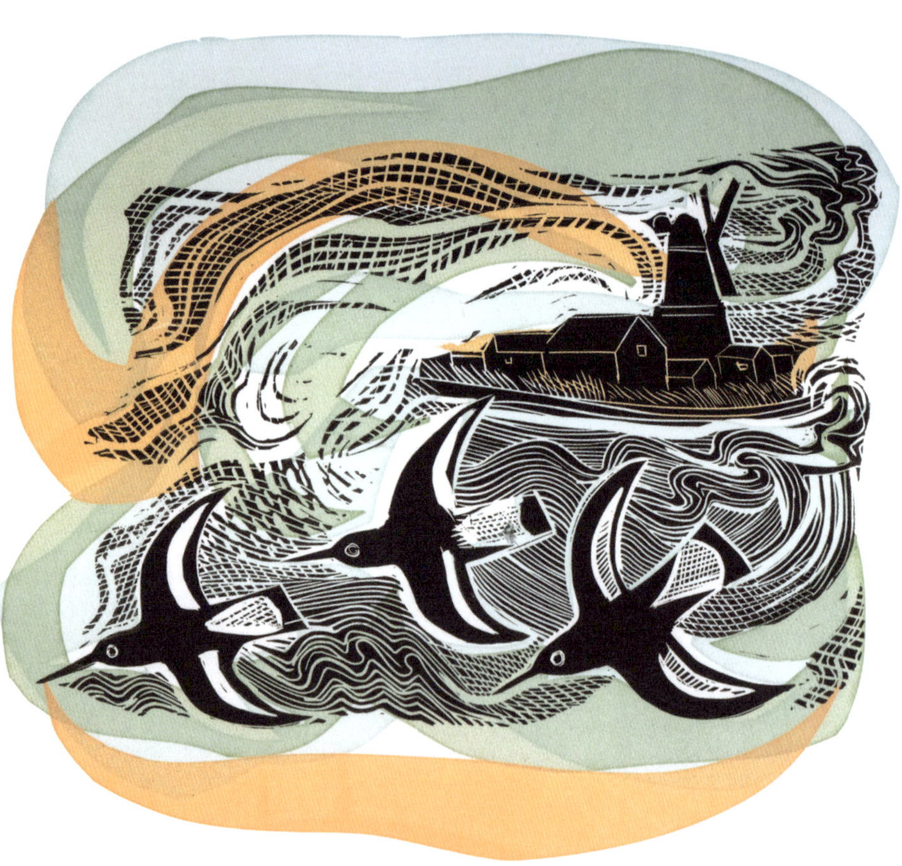

When I am away from home I like to cycle before breakfast; this is usually just as it is getting light. Last year I was staying in Great Walsingham in north Norfolk. On the last day of my stay, the early light that woke me promised another glorious day. I headed out on my bike down the beautiful winding road that led to the ford. My cycle ride came to an abrupt stop. Rising from the ford were thick rolls of mist which made the whole scene look like the setting for a P. D. James drama. It was not really fog but thick mist that spread out around the field, and as the sun rose the haunting mist disappeared.

Opposite:
Cley Windmill
(Linocut and silkscreen)

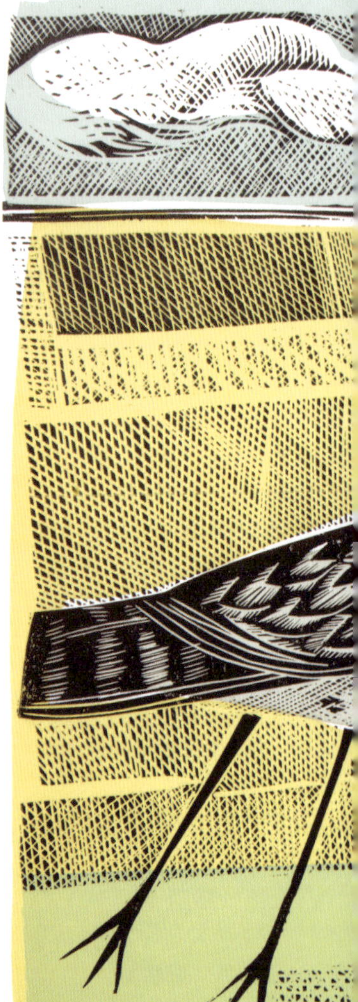

Much more than some of my other prints, *Norfolk Birds* demonstrates my great love of using line and pattern to create form. The birds guarding the egg are based on godwits and the background is Stiffkey beach, a vast area of sand on the North Norfolk coast. We have walked this beach many times and the changing colour and light on the sand is something I have endeavoured to portray in this print.

Opposite:
Norfolk Birds
(Linocut and silkscreen)

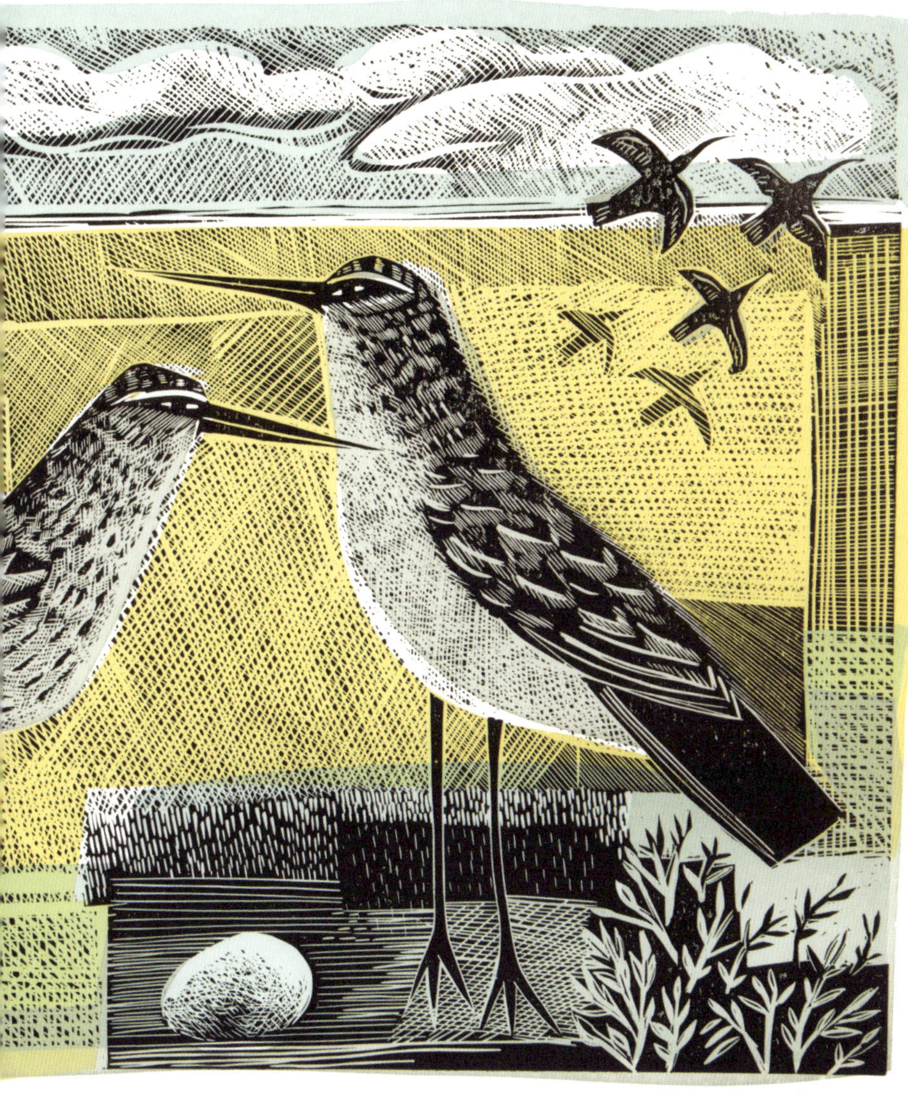

Southwold Harbour is one of our favourite ports of call. We usually moor up on the Walberswick pontoon as it is always quieter on that side of the harbour: no road, just fields and the coastal path that leads into Walberswick. Cattle graze in the fields beside the path and around them are white dots of egrets picking at insects thrown up by the cows' feet. The cattle egrets also appear alongside the boat and have the most fantastic yellow legs. They keep their heads amazingly still before darting forward to catch a fish. In the evening the fields fill with geese – large flocks of barnacle geese that fly in after spending the day inland. They announce their arrival with loud honking calls that seem to say, 'Watch out, low-flying geese approaching.'

Opposite:
Harbour Whippets
(Linocut and silkscreen)

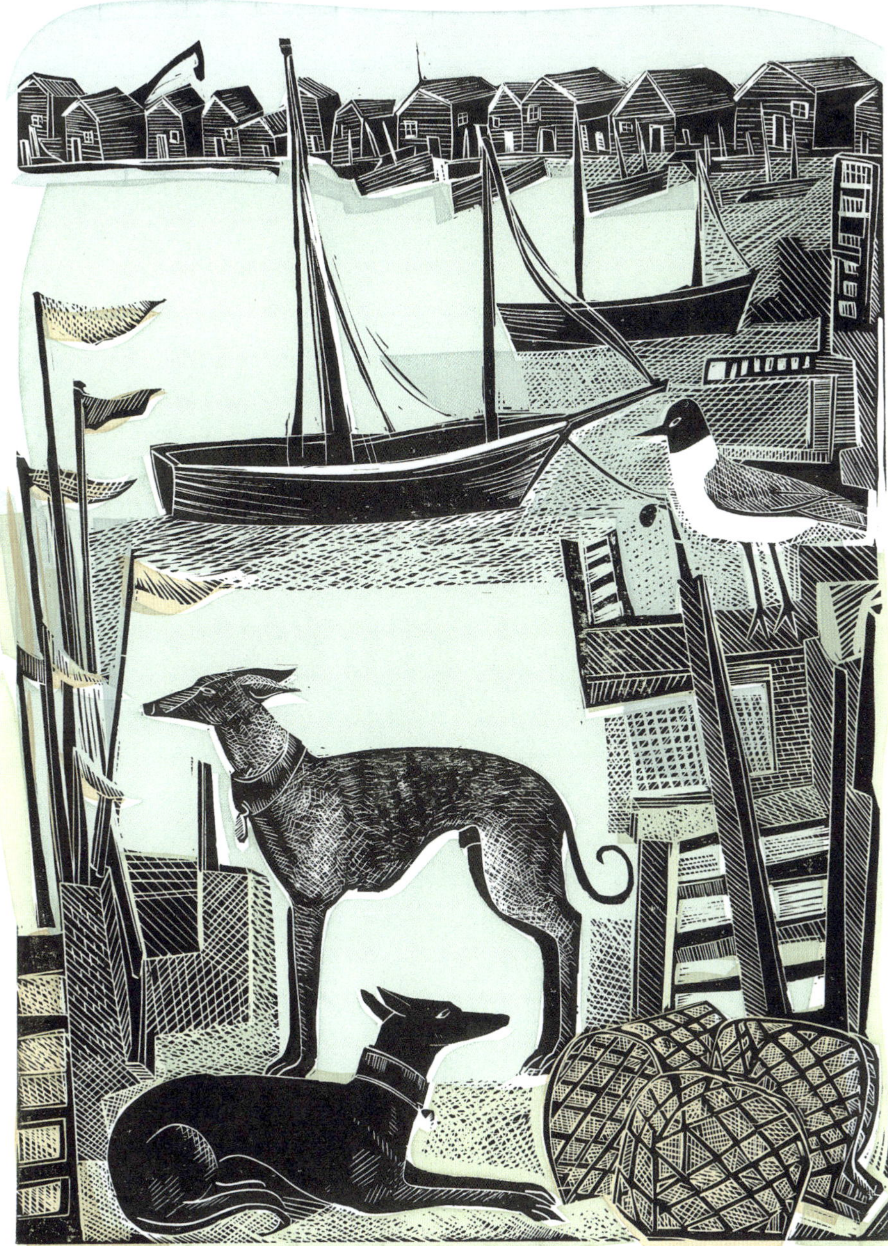

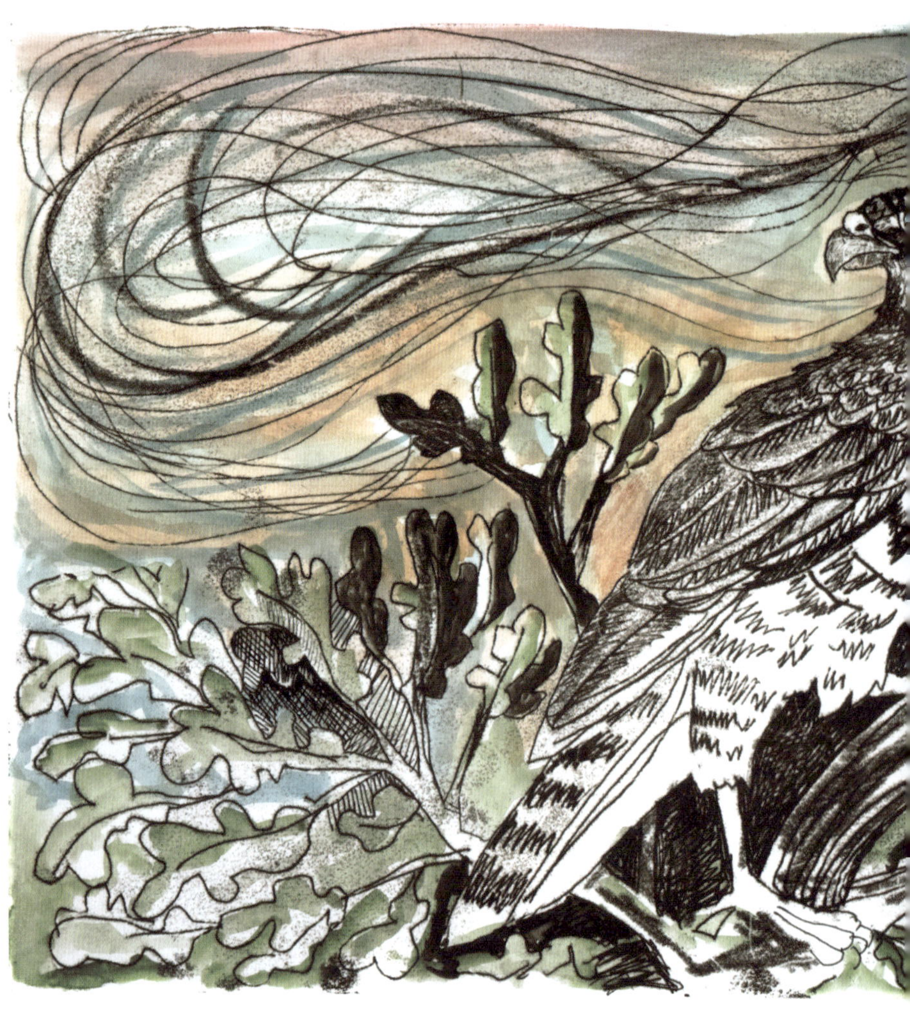

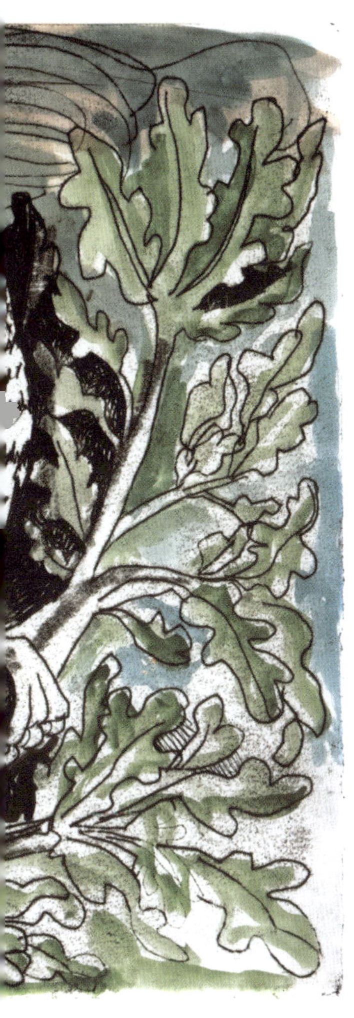

After breakfast when the day is still sharp and fresh, I take my whippet Oaty out for a walk. There is something about the rhythm of a morning walk, one footstep in front of another, that gets my brain in gear and ready for the day's work. Our walk usually takes us through the village and the small wood, which we call a spinney. The spinney has been subject to some rewilding and has a wildflower section in front of it. I try to always have my binoculars with me; one day I was lucky enough to see this sparrowhawk.

Opposite:
Sharp and Fresh
(Mono printing)

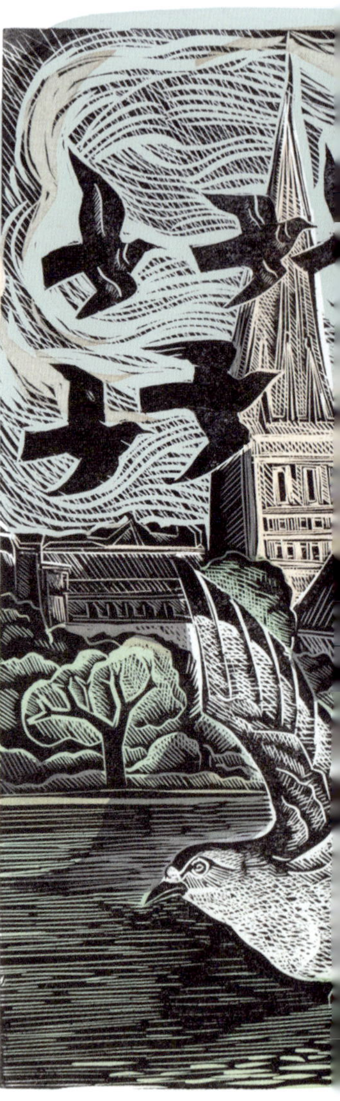

Cathedrals and churches have become breeding places for the peregrine falcon – All Saints Church in my local neighbourhood of Oakham has a breeding pair. The illustration here is a peregrine I saw in Norwich chasing its usual prey of pigeons. Their chosen town homes seem so different from the cliffs of Cornwall were I have watched them many times hunting rock doves and other small birds.

Opposite:
Peregrine and Pigeon
(Linocut and silkscreen)

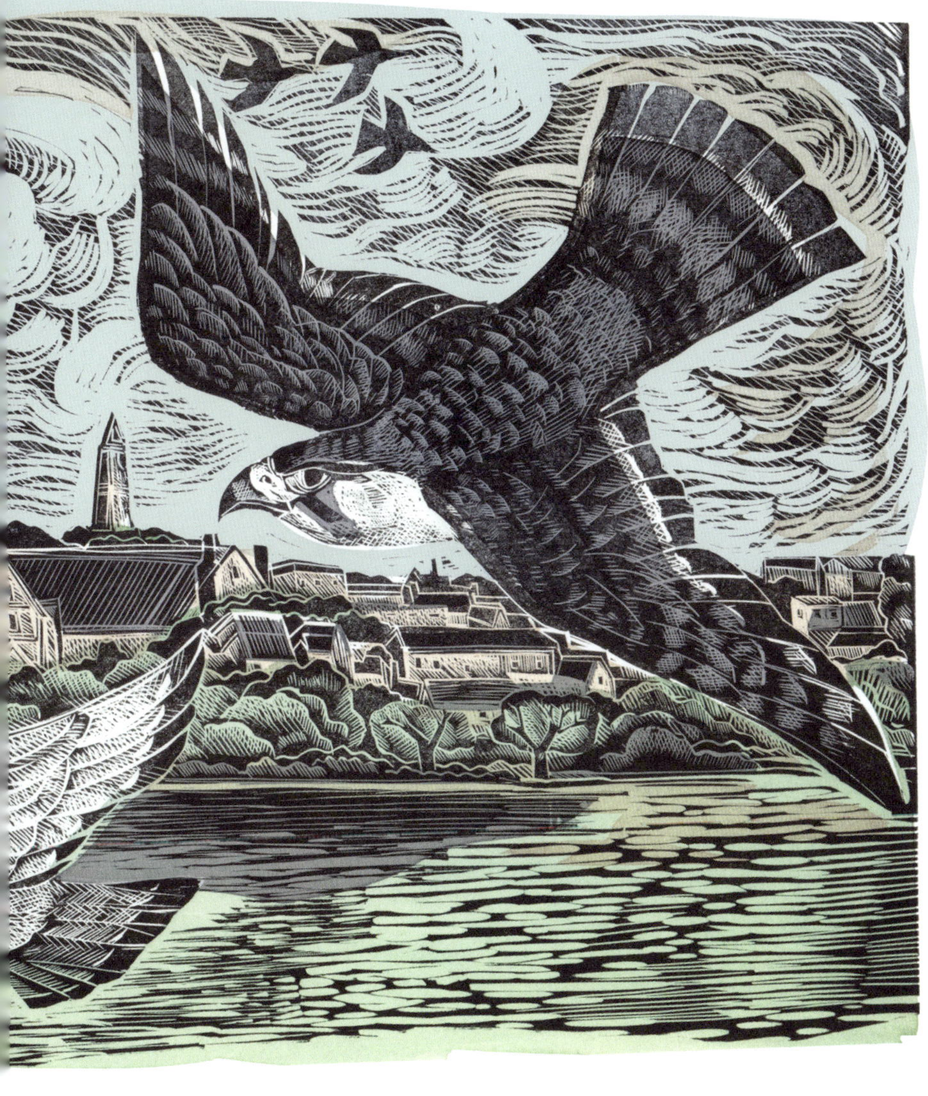

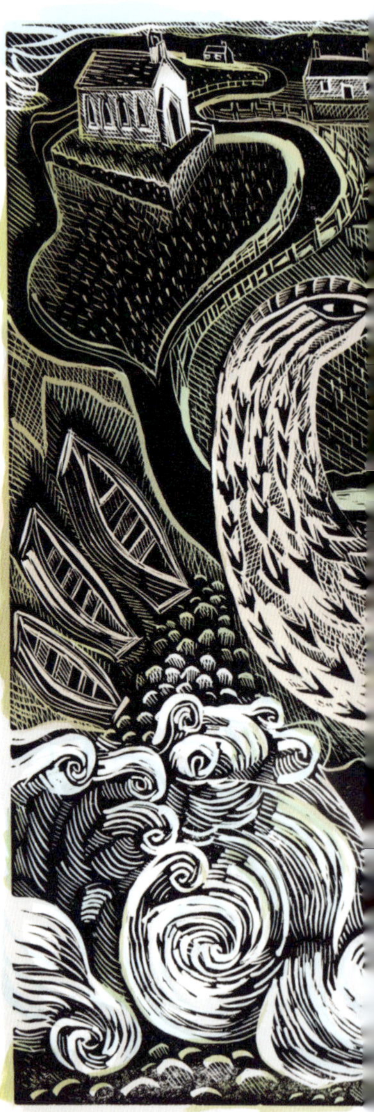

Fair Isle is an island of two opposite halves. The south of the island, pictured here, is where the people of Fair Isle live. It has green fields, wildflowers and bays encircling the sea. The north is rugged and wild, a place where the bonxies (great skuas) are on patrol. There is only one road, which runs from the north lighthouse to the south lighthouse, looping down to the Haven, a harbour bay of clear, turquoise water. The grassy slopes behind the Haven are the most beautiful place to sit and birdwatch. It is apt that this place is also where the bird observatory is housed, currently being rebuilt due to a fire. The rangers from the observatory are still on the island, now housed in the south lighthouse.

Opposite:
Fair Isle Curlews
(Linocut and silkscreen)

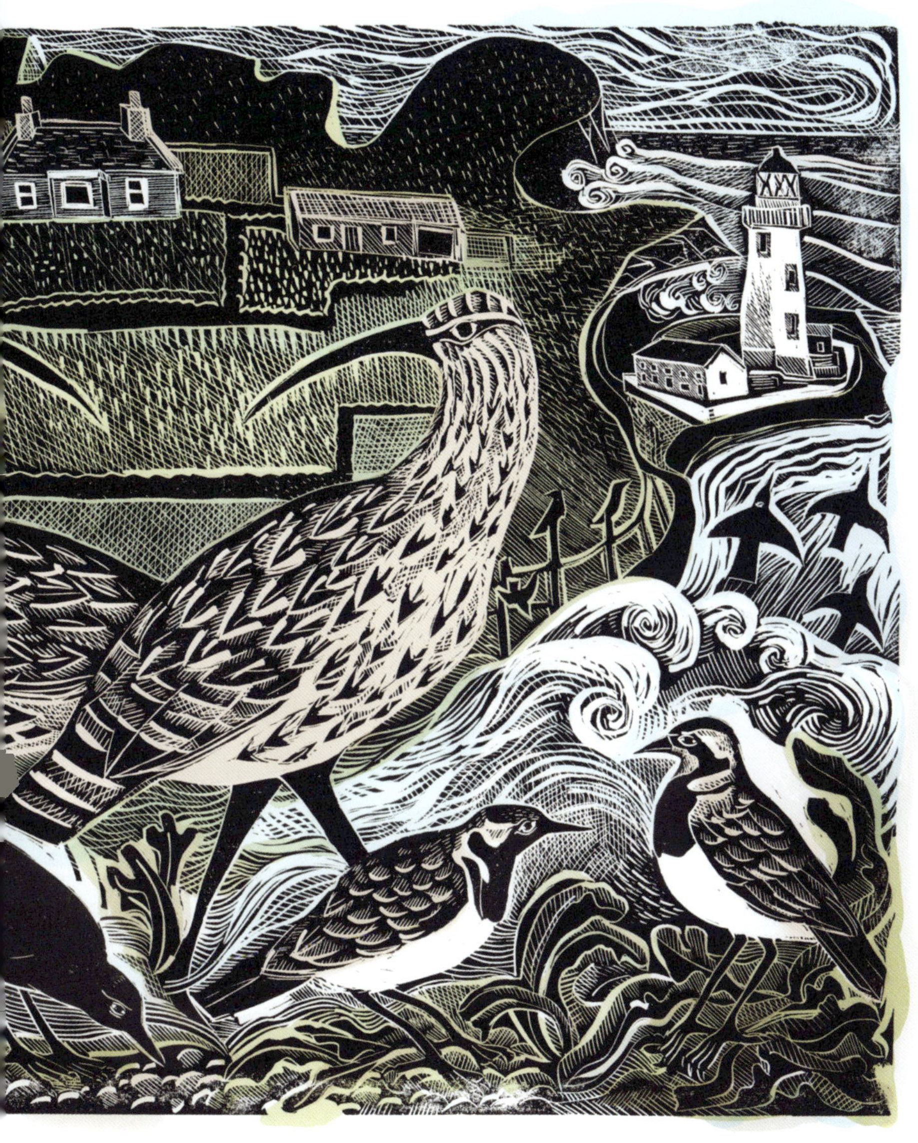

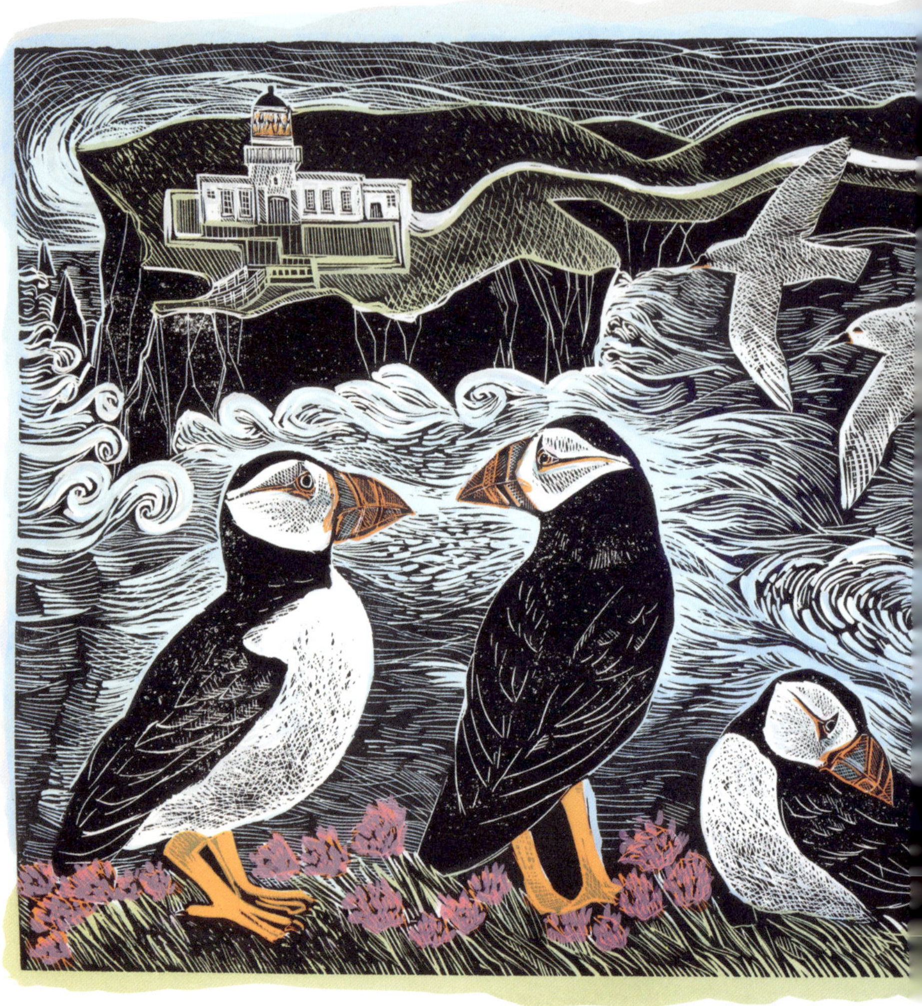

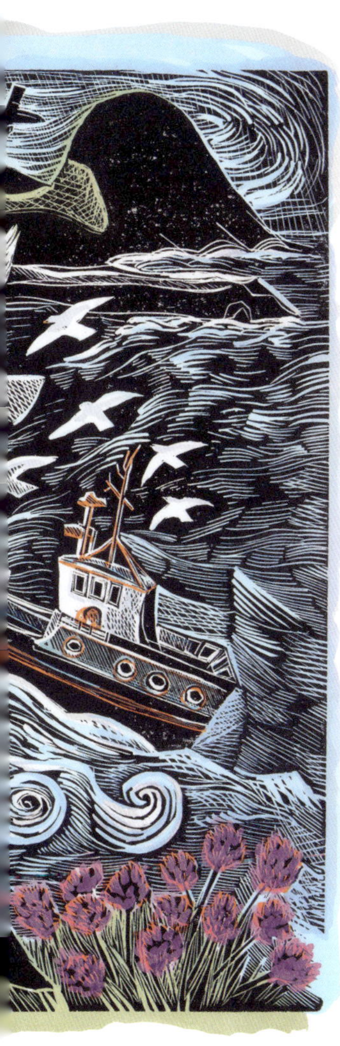

The north lighthouse is a squat version of the south lighthouse, its gleaming white tower only half the size. It was built to withstand the wild weather that has been thrown at it. This wild end of the island is a hunting ground for seals and orcas. The clifftops are fringed with puffins; their bright bills and orange feet are mesmerising to watch. Their flight is comical and their feet stretch out wide for incoming landing. Once on land they greet each other with cooing kisses and rubbing of bills. Their bright, stripy bills hold glistening silver fish that they have somehow lined up in straight rows ready to present to their mate and feed to their young.

Opposite:
Fair Isle Puffins
(Linocut and silkscreen)

The first time I saw Knepp Lake, it was bursting with energy and every corner I turned brought a fresh experience to inspire my artwork. I have tried to catch some of the energy of this scene in this print. In places the water is inky black where mature oak trees cast their shadows. There are thick reedbeds serving as hiding places for herons and dabbling ducks. There is the 'plop, plop' sound of coots diving, the 'tuck toot' of moorhens chatting. At the back of the lake a dead oak holds out skeleton branches decorated with cormorants, who stretch open their wings to dry in the setting sun. Large dragonflies dart across the surface of the water, evidence of the great biodiversity of this place.

Opposite:
Knepp Lake
(Linocut and silkscreen)

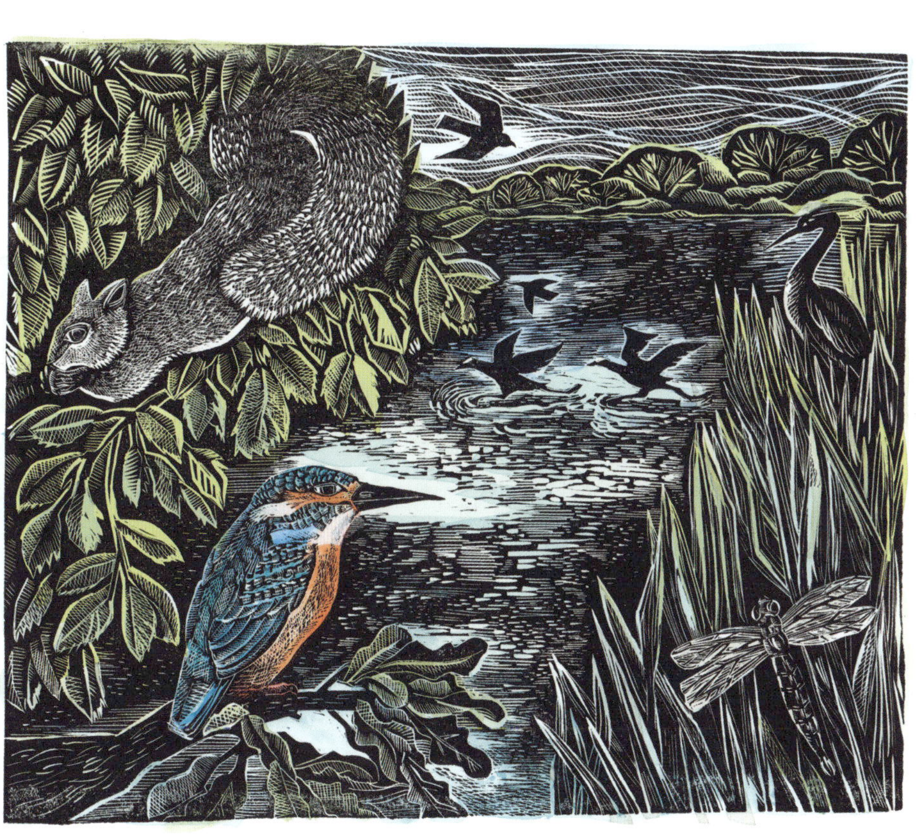

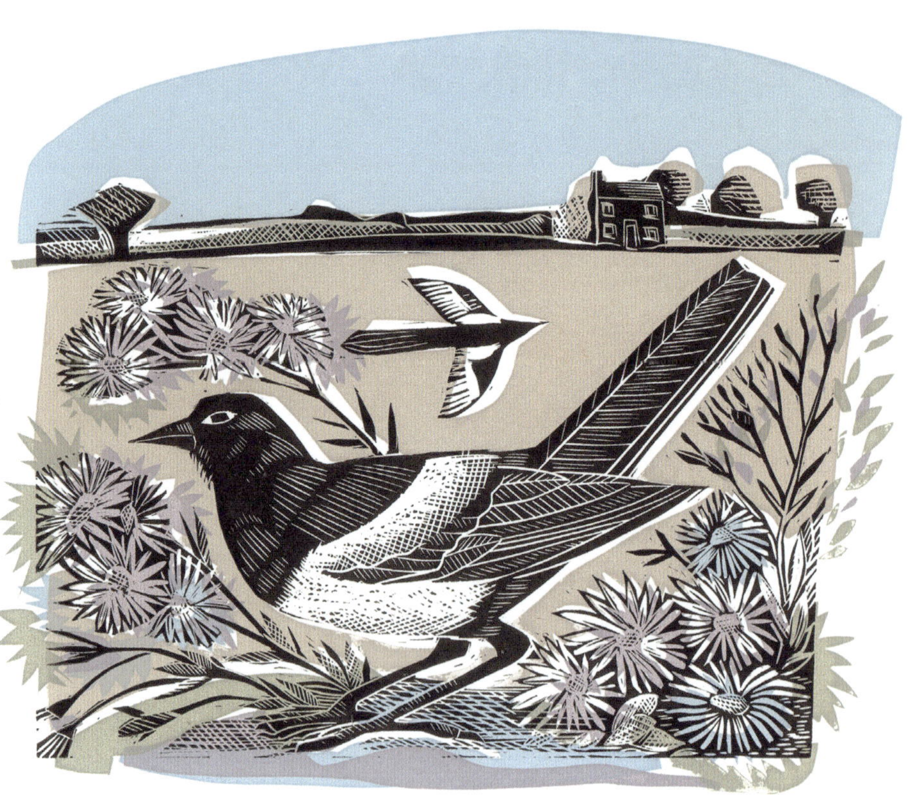

Opposite:
Two for Joy
(Linocut and silkscreen)

The magpie is a much maligned bird. Part of the crow family, it is considered by many to be vermin. I can never understand this; it's a bird of beauty and grace. It may steal eggs and be a predator but so do many other birds. So it remains a mystery to me why this is a hated bird. We have many in our village and it is still considered bad luck to see one. To dispel the bad luck, you are supposed to address the bird with the following words: "Oh Mr/ Mrs Magpie, what a beautiful bird you are, you are!"

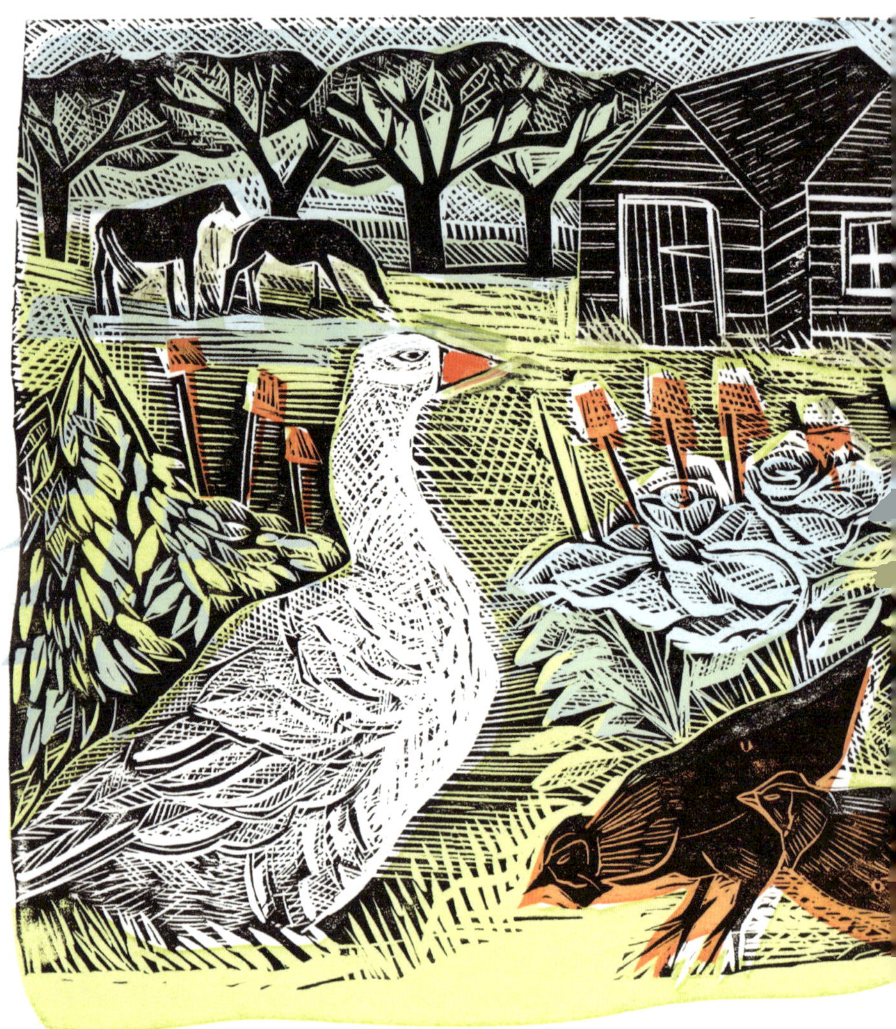

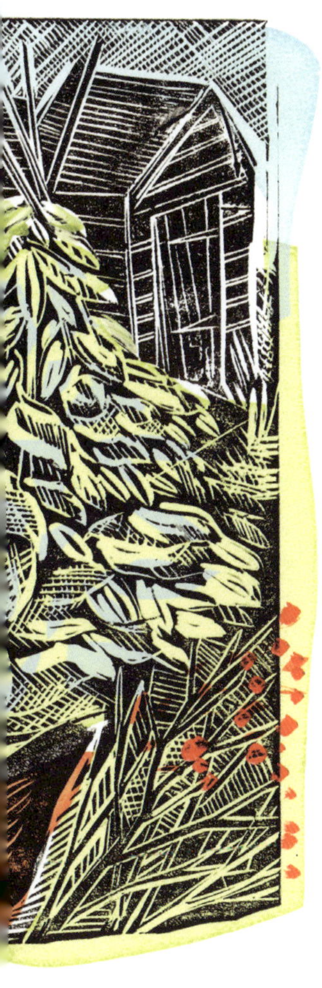

Above:
Wing Allotments
(Linocut and silkscreen)

The allotments near our home are a beautiful scramble of sheds and neat rows of vegetables. The small patchwork plots are the first thing you see when you enter Wing. For a short while, Mark and I had a half-allotment there which we endeavoured to tend. It was a wonderful experience to be up early and to walk through the empty lanes of our village to the allotment, the first light of the day shining through windowpanes of tumbledown greenhouses and spreading out like fingers across the soil plots. Each plot reflected the village character who tended it and I am sorry to say that our plot reflected our own characters!

This is an illustration of Arctic terns created for Miranda Krestovnikoff's book *RSPB Birds*. Arctic terns have the longest migration of all birds: a round trip of up to 35,000 kilometres (that's 22,000 miles each year.) They feed in shallow coastal waters on small fish and sand eels, and nest on beaches and small offshore islands. I have watched Arctic terns on Fair Isle; they return there each year to breed. You know you have found the Arctic terns' nest site by the noise. They make their presence felt by great squawking above your head and divebombing, making you well aware to watch your step.

Opposite:
Terns at Sea
(Linocut and silkscreen)

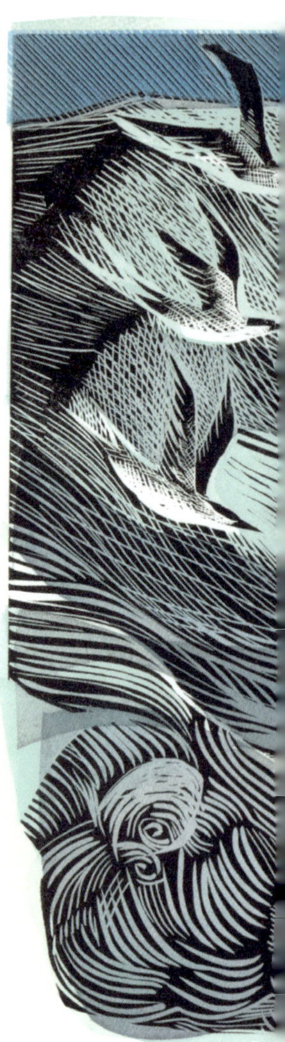

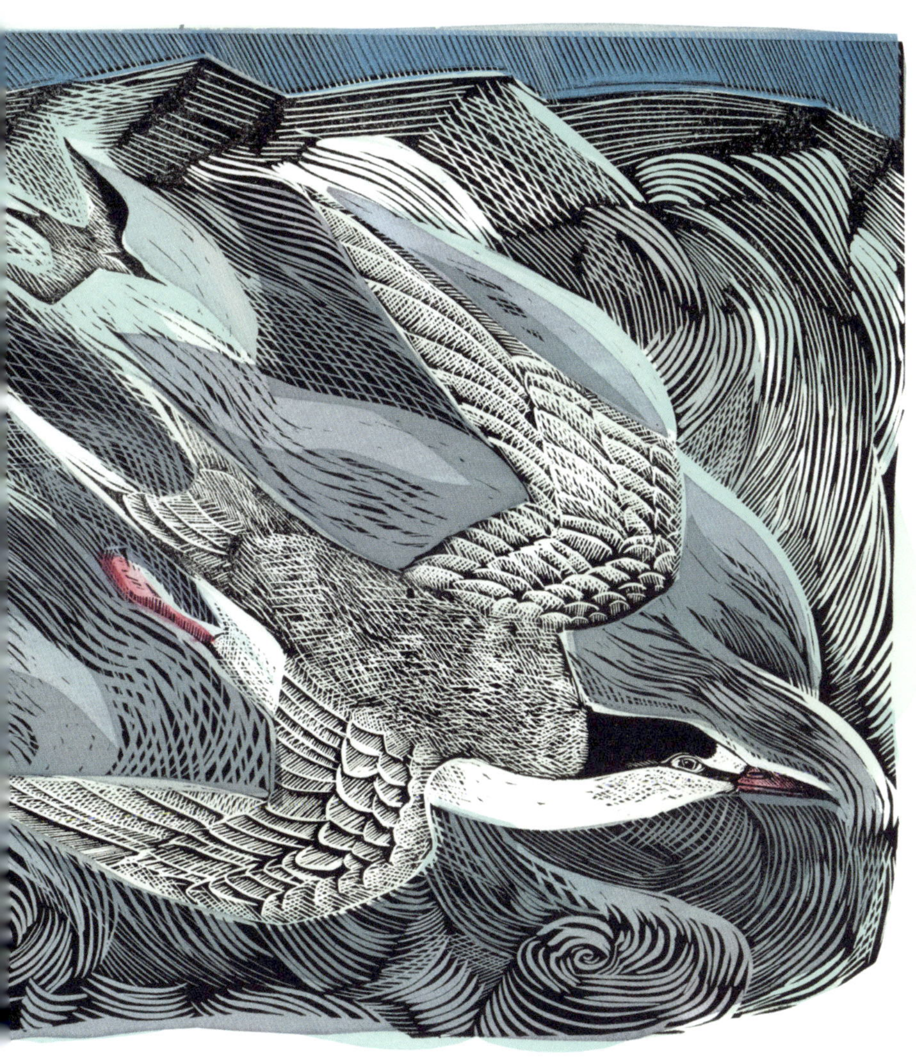

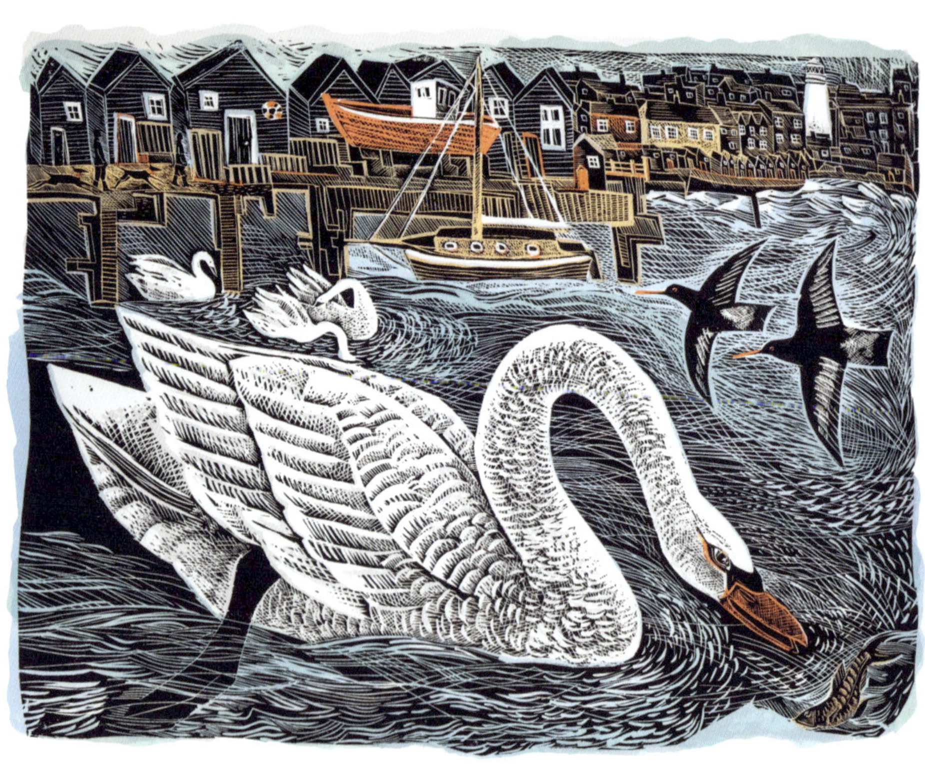

Every summer we take *Windsong* to Southwold Harbour. It is a day's sail from Martlesham Creek, so it is the first port of call after the winter. We use the Walberswick side of the river. The view on one side of the boat is of cow fields and reedbeds; on the other it is the wide river, Southwold town and a lighthouse in the distance. We enjoy many aspects of boat life but waking up onboard *Windsong* is hard to beat. The birds come into view through the round portholes, which frame the landscape, giving you a concentrated version of the view outside.

Opposite:
Southwold Swan
(Linocut and silkscreen)

Shooting Stars was originally commissioned some years back by BBC *Countryfile* magazine, for an article about walking the countryside at night without using artificial light. The writer described how, without a torch, your eyes quickly become accustomed to the dark. Then, if we keep still and quiet, nature will come to us. In this case the writer was lying in a grassy field watching shooting stars. He had kept so still that a young hare leaped straight over him. I have not had the experience of a hare leaping over me, but I have seen shooting stars, most often in our garden. We are lucky in Wing to have low light pollution so on late summer nights we can witness the most beautiful displays of one shooting star after another.

Opposite:
Shooting Stars
(Linocut and silkscreen)

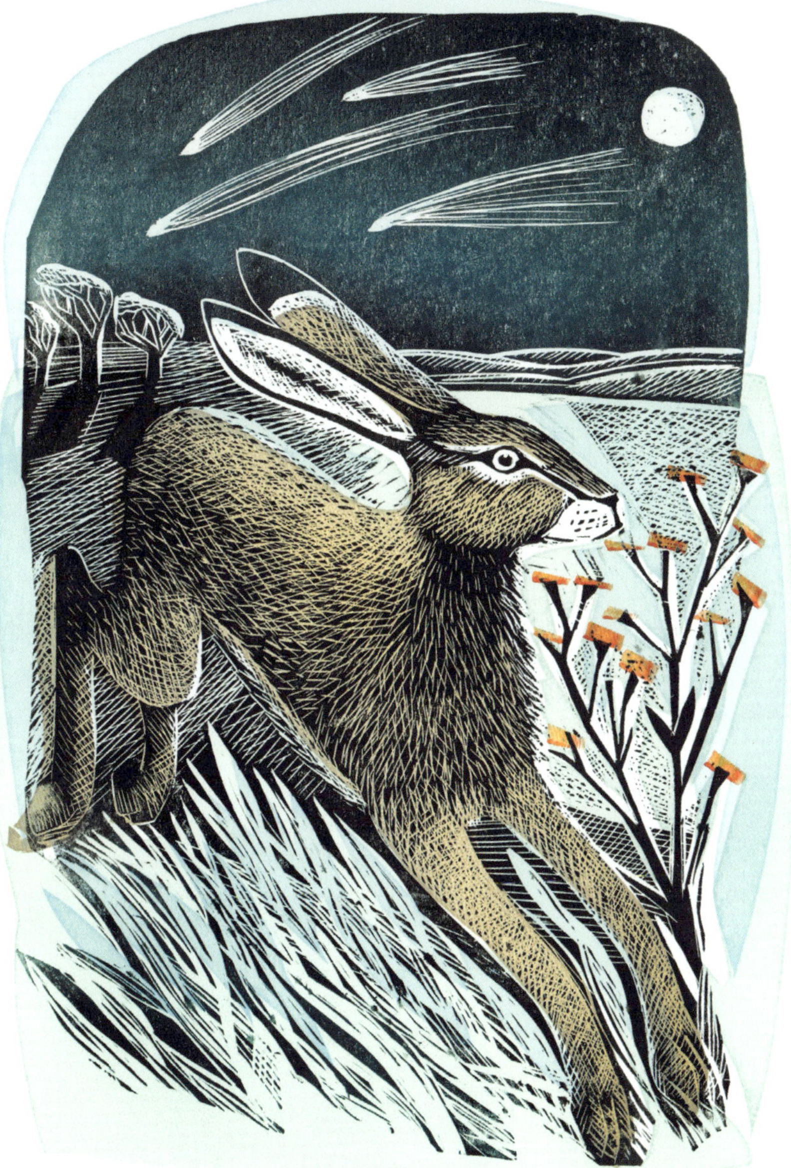

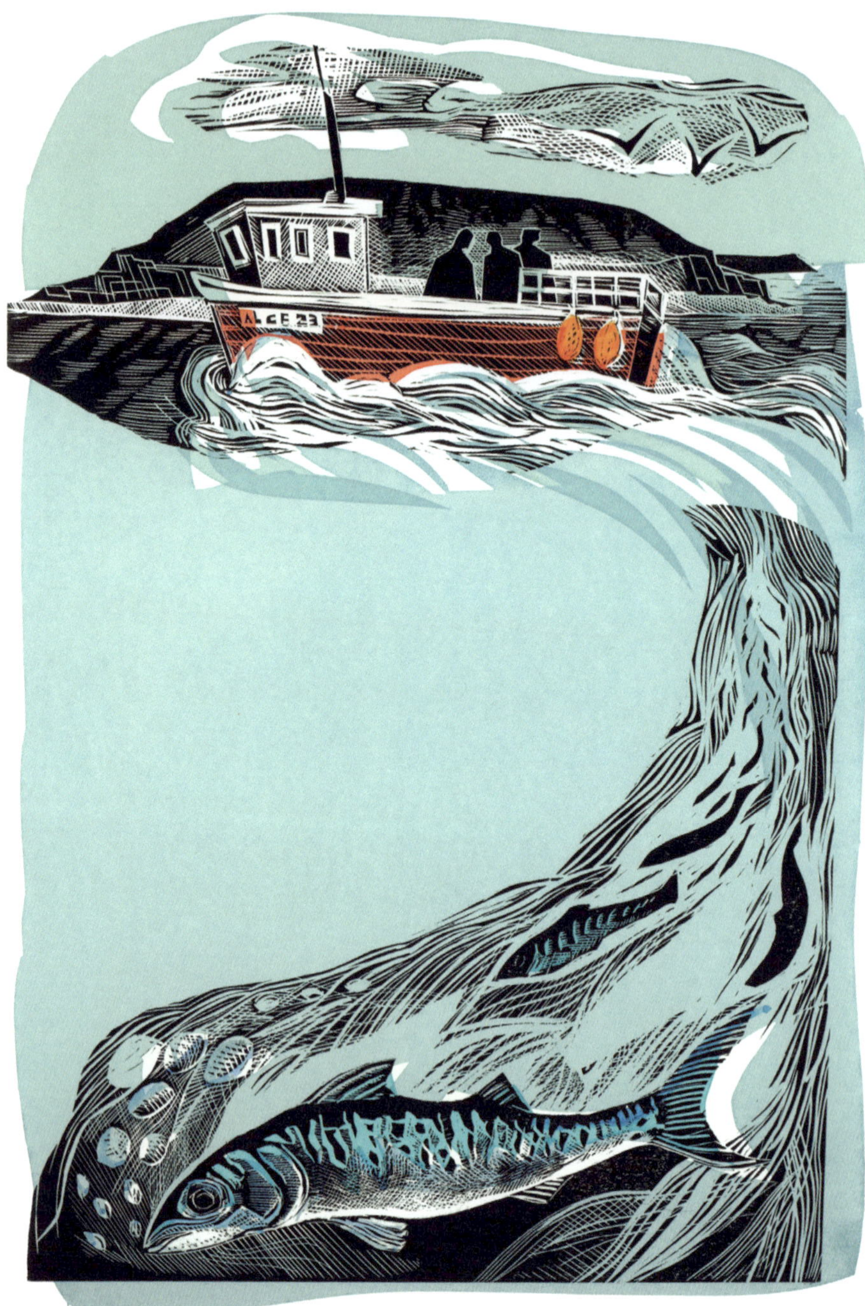
ALCE 23

During the summer, Mark and I visit many harbours along the UK coastline. Some of these still have working fishing fleets. These tend to be the harbours I like the best; they are full of character. I enjoy the mess of ropes, lobster pots, flags and fishing nets. When we're sleeping on board *Windsong*, you hear the fishing vessels leaving the harbour in the early hours.

Opposite:
Mackerel and Boat
(Linocut and silkscreen)

Amble Marina, in Northumberland, has the twin benefits of being a comfortable place to sort the boat and having great birdlife. We head out from here to visit Croquet Island, a bird reserve where roseate terns nest. You are not allowed on to the island, but when sailing close by, you can hear the squeals and calls and see the white clouds of birds that have claimed this small island. Puffins gather at its edges, alongside basking seals. The seals in the sea bob up, curious to see who is passing by.

Opposite:
Puffin Lighthouse and Boat
(Linocut and silkscreen)

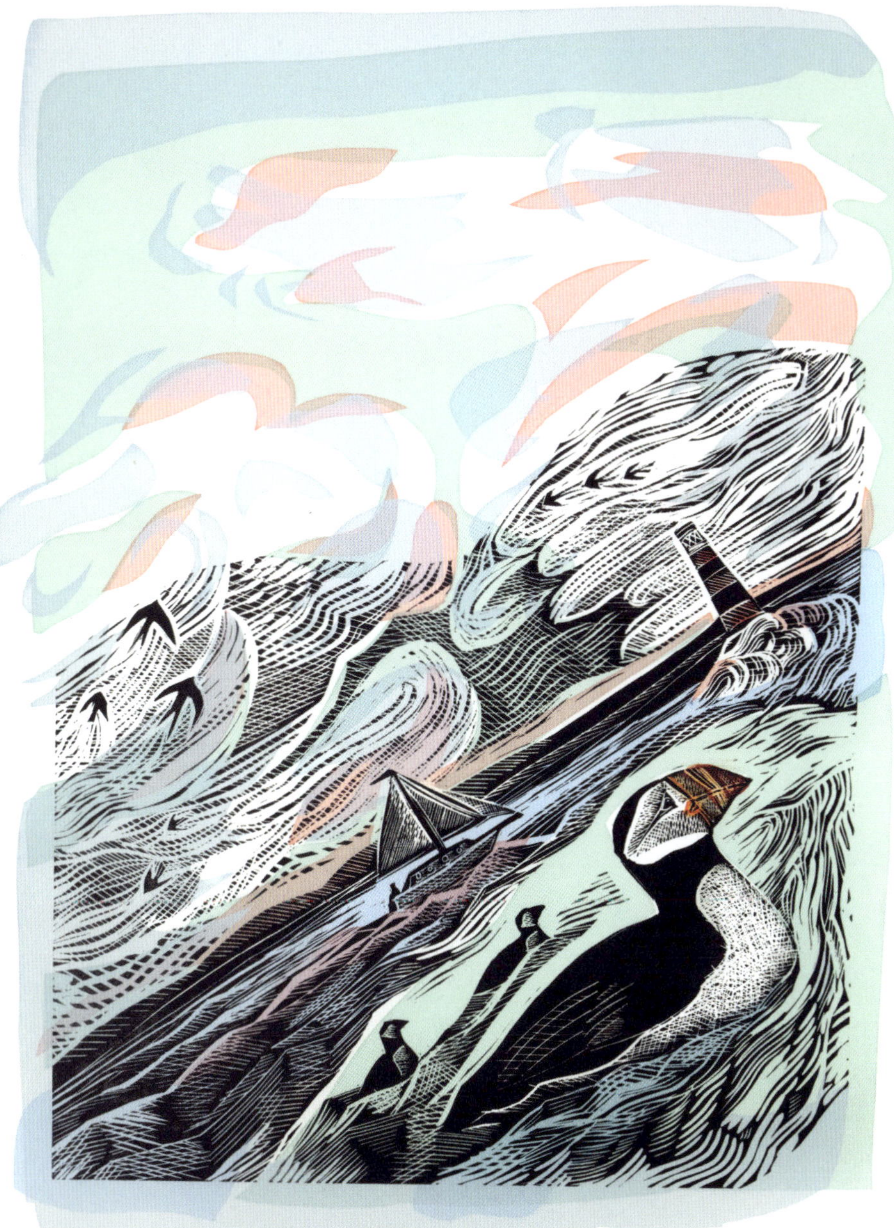

This print was done at a point when I was moving from intaglio printmaking to relief work. It is very simply cut and is more about colour; it attempts to capture a summer feeling of heat and a clear blue sky. This is very much a simplified depiction of seeing ringed plovers in Suffolk some years back; the plover is a bird I love very much. They are usually in small groups, their plumage buff brown with a sharp band of black. These colours make them blend into the stony seashore's edge. This helps to protect them from predators, particularly when nesting.

Opposite:
Summer Plover
(Linocut and silkscreen)

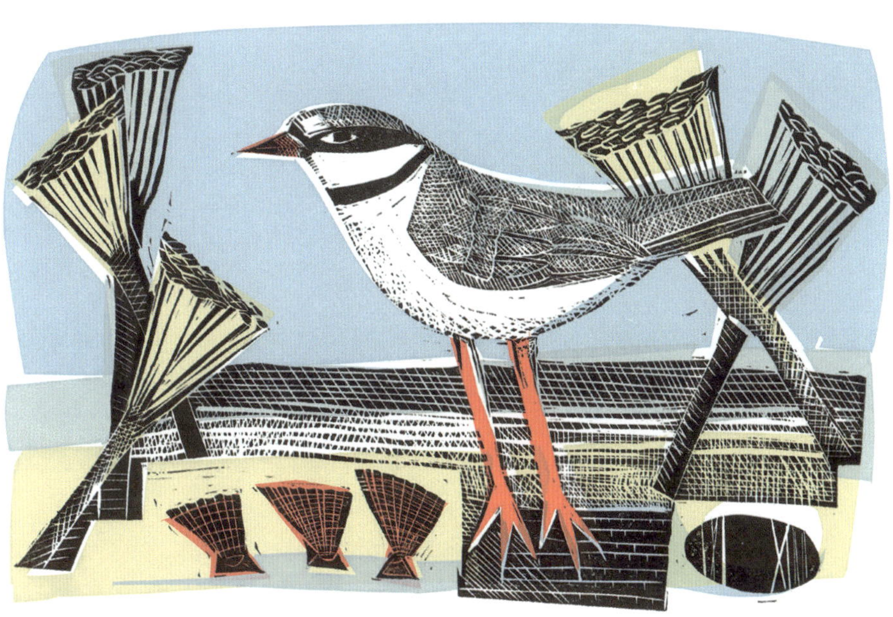

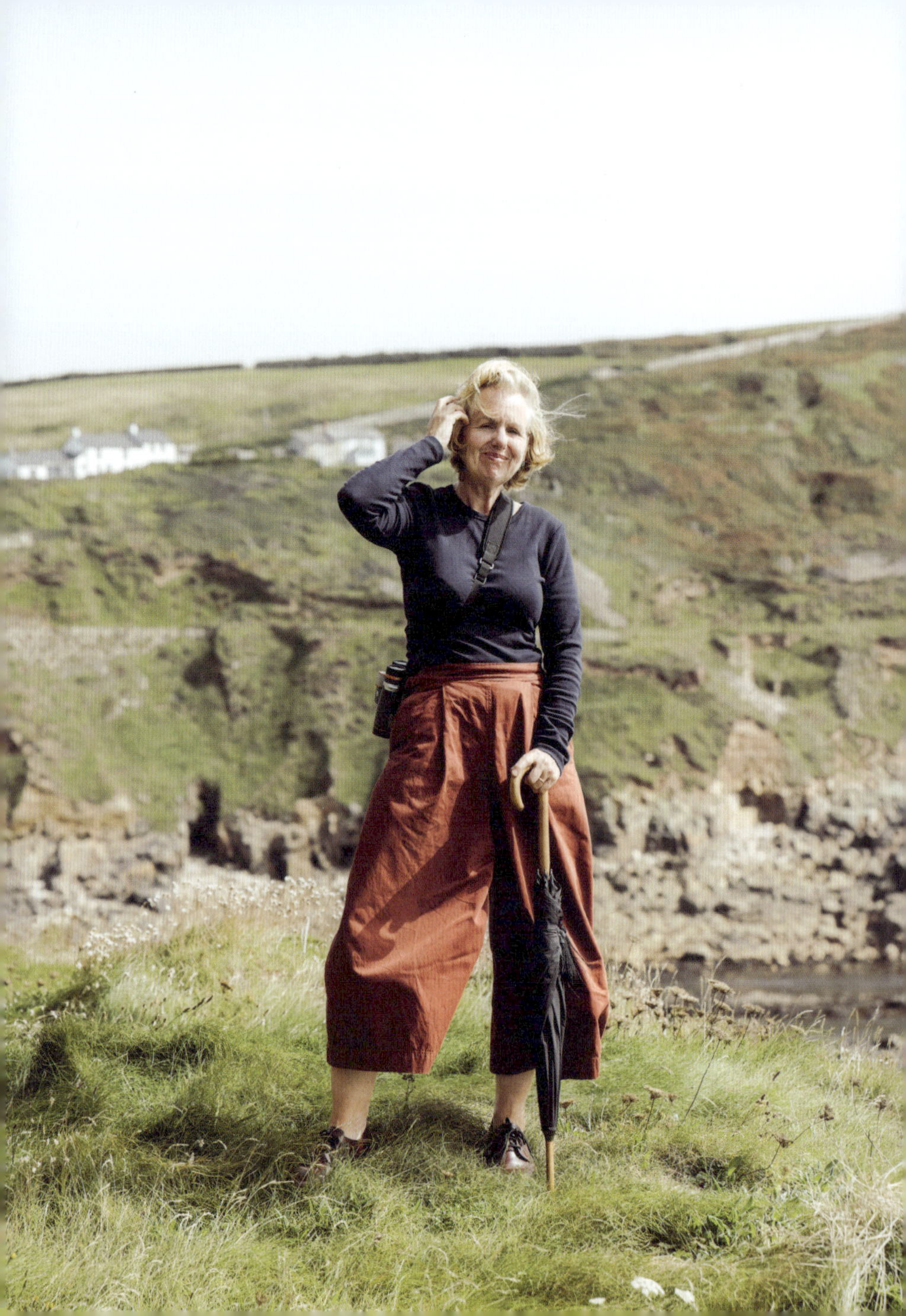

About the Author

ANGELA HARDING lives in the small county of Rutland and works out of the studio at the bottom of her garden in the village of Wing.

Angela has worked on the covers for a number of books including P. D. James, Ted Hughes, Katya Balen and James Rebanks. Her children's book *RSPB Birds* by Miranda Krestovnikoff was longlisted for the Klaus Flugge prize. Her most recent children's book *Wilding*, by Isabella Tree, was shortlisted for the 2024 Wainwright Prize for Children's Writing on Nature and Conservation. Other recent publications include *Blossomise* by Simon Armitage, a *Sunday Times* bestseller.

Angela has written and illustrated three books published by Little, Brown: *A Year Unfolding*, *Wild Light* and *Still Waters & Wild Waves*.

Angela's unique and distinct style has become instantly recognisable to nature lovers and book lovers alike. Her fans flock to buy her merchandise including calendars, cards, tea towels, tote bags and jigsaws.

She was the 2024 artist for the 'Books Are My Bag' tote bag, celebrating independent bookshops across the UK and Ireland.

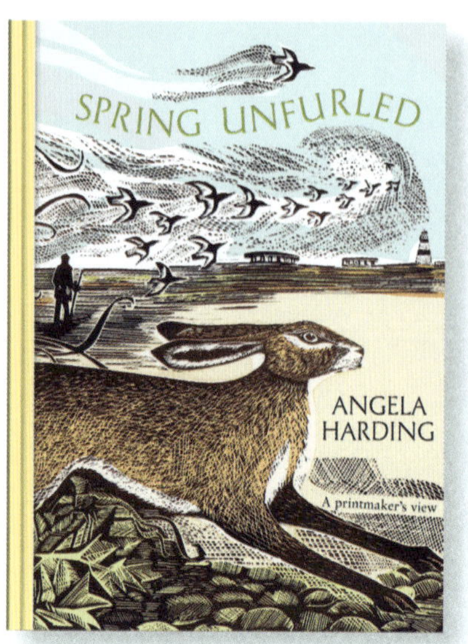

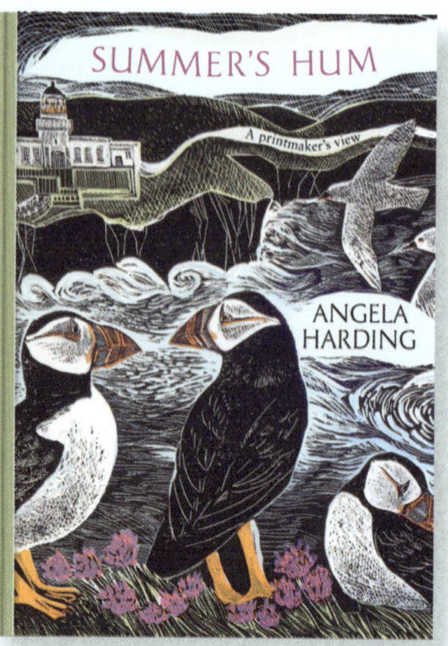

Collect the full Seasonal Quartet series

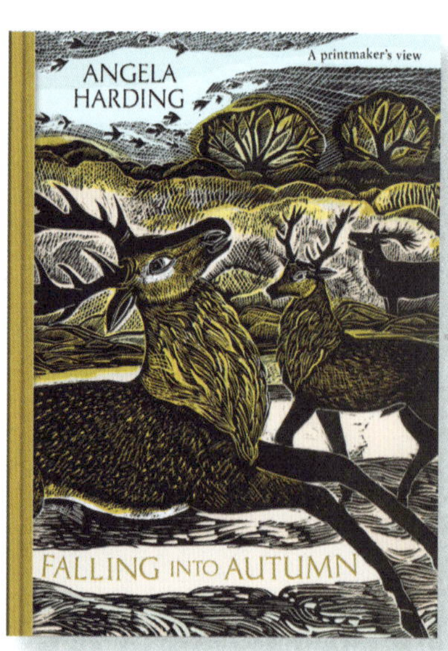

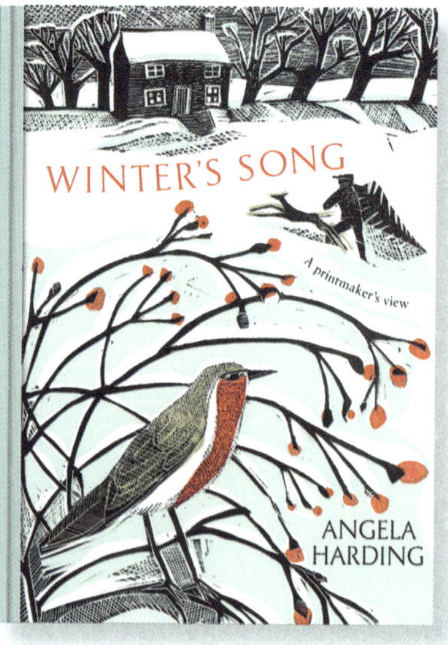

If you enjoyed *Summer's Hum*, explore Angela's other books with Little, Brown

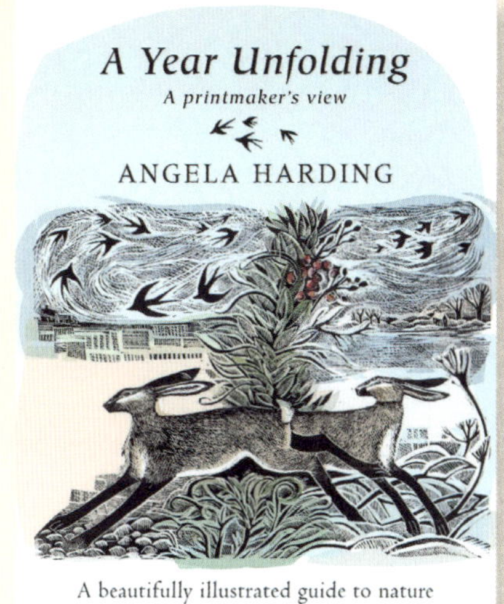

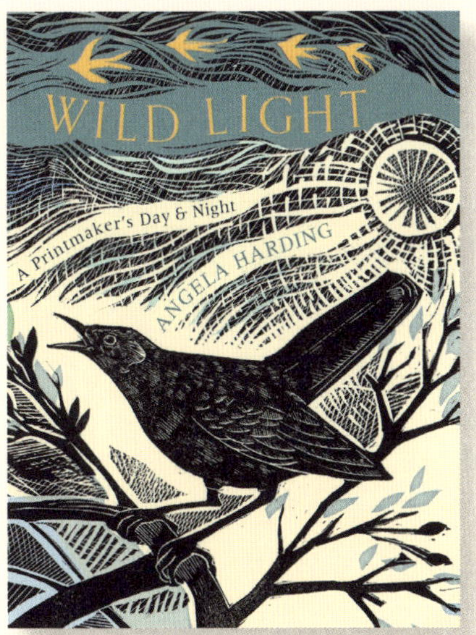

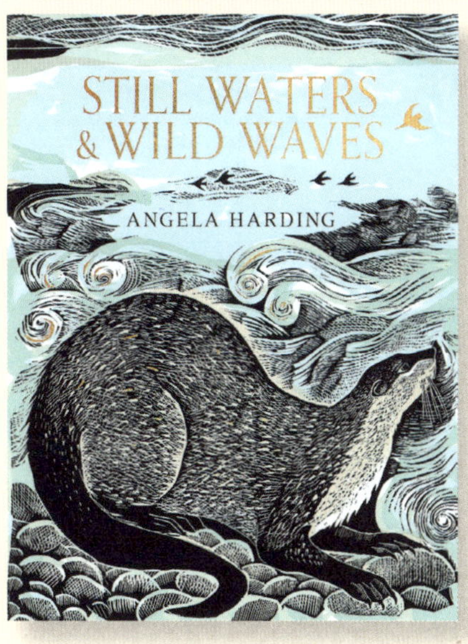

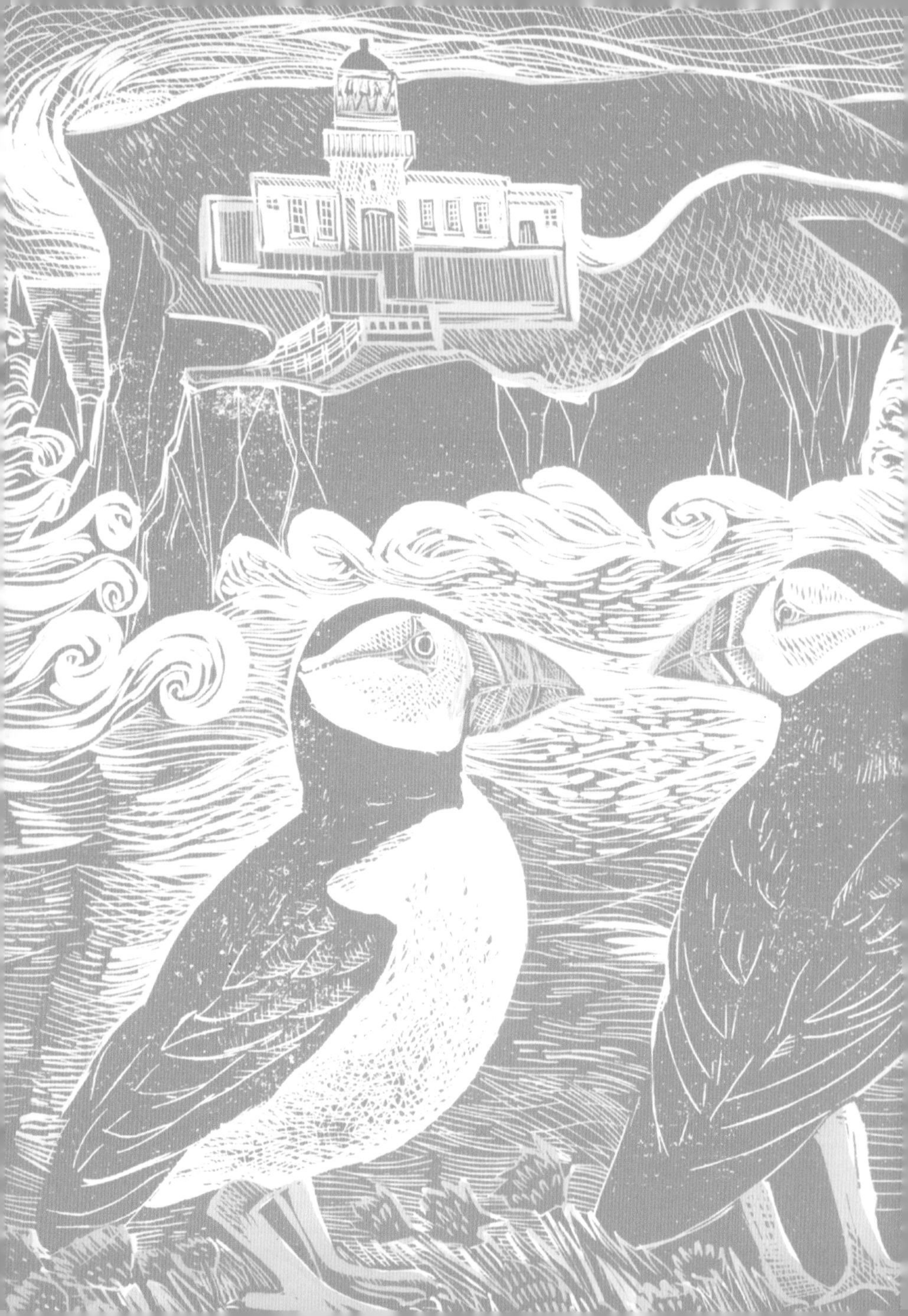